Troubled Lovers in History

A Sequence of Poems

Albert Goldbarth

Ohio State University Press

Columbus

Copyright © 1999 by The Ohio State University.
All rights reserved.

Library of Congress Cataloging-in-Publication Data

Goldbarth, Albert.
    Troubled lovers in history : a sequence of poems / Albert
Goldbarth.
        p.   cm.
    ISBN 0-8142-0813-4 (cloth : alk. paper). — ISBN 0-8142-5015-7
(alk. paper)
    I. Title.
PS3557.O354T76   1999
811'.54—dc21   98-39035
                                                    CIP

Text and jacket design by Paula Newcomb.
Type set in Usherwood by Tseng Information Systems.
Printed by Thomson-Shore, Inc.

The paper used in this publication meets the minimum
requirements of the American National Standard for
Information Sciences—Permanence of Paper for
Printed Library Materials. ANSI Z 39.48-1992.

9 8 7 6 5 4 3 2 1

ACKNOWLEDGMENTS

The author is grateful to the editors of the following journals for first providing the poems in this collection a home:

The Alaska Review: Substratum
The Bellingham Review: In the Bar in the Bar
The Beloit Poetry Journal: Natural History
Black Warrior Review: Travel Notes
Boulevard: "*Of Course* They're Strangers. They *Aren't Me.*"
Crab Orchard Review: There, Too
The Georgia Review: Imps
The Gettysburg Review: Against; Two Weeks, with Polo Chorus
The Iowa Review: Dog, Fish, Shoes (or Beans); The Number of Utterly Alien
    Civilizations in *Star Trek* and *Star Wars*
The Kenyon Review: ***!!!The Battle of the Century!!!***; The Fiction Shelf; In
Ontario Review: Con Carne
Poetry: Ancestored-Back Is the Overpresiding Spirit of This Poem; True;
    Various Ulia
Poetry Northwest: Alternative Uses
Quarterly West: Complete with Starry Night and Bourbon Shots; Directional; "Duo
    Tried Killing Man with Bacon"; *The Lost Continent* (1951); Squash and Stone;
    What We're Used To

and for reprinting certain of these poems:

The Best American Poetry 1997: Complete with Starry Night and Bourbon Shots
Harper's: Ancestored-Back Is the Overpresiding Spirit of This Poem
Poetry Daily: Dog, Fish, Shoes (or Beans); "*Of Course* They're Strangers. They
    Aren't Me."

and a special thanks to Mindy Wilson at *Black Warrior Review* for using "Travel Notes" in that journal's chapbook series

and, for other special editorial generosities, thanks to David Baker, Susan Burton, Stan Lindberg, Joel Lovell, Pattiann Rogers, Margot Schilpp, Marion Stocking; and to Ellen Satrom, for her fine eye.

These poems attempt to look at what we've learned by this time in our century to call "relationships" (romantic/marital relationships for the most part, although the section titled "Generations" includes poems about child and parents). Their group notion is that the ups and downs of our contemporary hearts can be amplified by historic reference: from the *Travels of Marco Polo* to the hokey delights of 1950s horror films, "othertime" attempts to speak with, and for, *our* time. There is, necessarily, a good deal of estrangement and bickering in these pieces, and much of human components that won't happily cohere; but in between are small moments meant to be more idyllic, and *those* of course are

for Skyler.

The most beautiful of pairings come from opposition. . . .
Consider the bow and the lyre.

    —Heracleitus

CONTENTS

travel notes

Travel Notes

introductory section

This sad first line presents somebody
sitting at the window, in her seventh year of marriage,
in a fall of early morning light
so new—so yet untouched by any texture—
it's incapable of artifice:
everything shows. And so
her disappointments and frailties
are obvious in this introductory section
—in the way her hopes of seven years ago are on display,
are an unmediated beaming, in the photograph
she keeps on the credenza ledge.
And by the space between these two far faces
we can measure a journey, something
like the passage that Monet provides his haystacks.
—Not in miles; but in deepness
over time. —And not in shoeleather,
no; but hour by hour, sun by cloud,
in the ripening weight of experience.

1.

"A new day's march, the tins of biscuit gone
last night to thieves. So be it. We wade
through our fatigue as if it were only another
infested stream to cross. . . ."
                                    Wait: Did he say
only? "Oh, that. That's merely Bloodsucker Creek."
"That's just Deathrattle Canyon."
Ambling casually across the leechy muckholes
of this scary planet, humming *Rule Britannia.* . . .
"To his credit, he uttered no word of regret."

The greatest travelers never kvetch. For them,
the application of potentially fatal Saharan heat
to flesh is—"vigorating," one called it.
How can you be something so sublime,
so *monumentally* sublime, as "stoic,"
if needles of ice *won't* work their way into your feet,
if swarms of stinger-gnats *won't* boil up
out of the jungle brush as thickly as spewed-up gruel?
"This proved a tonic, after our days of restful confinement."
Adversity burnishes them to perfection.

So: in 1887, thirst reduces the robust party of British explorer
Sir Francis Younghusband to the extremity
of lapping the blood of a freshly beheaded rooster,
then of a throat-slit sheep ("immediately it coagulated
into a cake"), and finally "Islam and Yoldi
collected camel's urine, mixed it with sugar and vinegar,
held their noses, and drank." By night they struggle ahead.
By day they bury one another up to the gizzard in sand,
for the feeble extra degrees of its cool. Eventually the thirst
"did not torment us, as it had done . . .
for the mouth-cavity had become as dry as the outside skin,
and the craving was dulled."
                                    And what *is*
Younghusband's summary? "It is a curious fact,
but when real difficulties seem to be closing around,
one's spirits rise . . . difficulties seem only to make you
more and more cheery." Somewhere else,
concomitantly, an arctic adventurer rolls
the rotted soles off his feet as if peeling a tangerine.

"There was, of course, some initial discomfort
as we kept on toward our goal."
Of course. Of such intrepid mettle
are the High Lords and Ladies of Wanderlust.

                                                              But

                    ~

I prefer the more roundedly human touch
of a grandiose sniveler, who *knows* an inconvenience
when he sees one, and vituperates it accordingly.
Thomas Manning is a nineteenth-century master
of this arch effect. "Turning my head back towards the west,
I had a noble view of a set of snowy mountains
collected into focus, empurpled with the evening sun. . . .
I heartily wished I might never see them again."
His room in Phari-dzong, on the road to Lhasa,
is "low, long, dark, narrow, windowless, full of smoke.
Dirt, dirt, grease. Misery." Simply: "I find going uphill
does not agree with me."
                            Or Dickens, on his first night
in a canal boat through the Alleghenies:
"I found suspended on either side of the cabin,
three long tiers of hanging book-shelves, designed apparently
for volumes of the small octavo size. Looking
with greater attention, I descried on each shelf
a sort of microscopic sheet and blanket; and then
I began dimly to comprehend that the passengers
were the library, and that they were to be arranged,
edge-wise, on these shelves, till morning."
Of tobacco juice and its being so freely spat, and
of the various "zephyr whisperings" that emanate their richness
from the other thirty beds, he rises to rhetoric
impassioned and ornate enough to otherwise be chronicling
the battle of Masada or our touchdown on the moon.

Well what does Dickens *expect?* "Have got a diarrhoea,"
Byron says in one of his earlier letters, "and bites from the mosquitoes.
But what of that?
Comfort must not be expected by folks that go a pleasuring."

2.

When his eyes can focus, my brother-in-law is lost
in reading a book about the European mapping of Australia
—sandstorms; sunsets like a smear of iodine dye;
bone-jangling thunderstorms; betrayals.
When his eyes can focus. . . .
                                        Sometimes, though,
the M.S. won't allow that small coherence;
much less walking. Then a day is a matter
of thought and dream; and of the half-state progeny
of thought and dream; and there are places
wholly independent of geography and time,
to which we'll spirit ourselves.
And surely if a man can exit
his skull without anywhere shattering it,
the roof of a house on Nathan Road in Edgemoor, Illinois,
is no impediment, nor the sunlit, swaddling
atmosphere of Earth.

∼

" 'On what am I walking?' she asks.
And the table replies: 'On a world—Mars.' "
This is the seance of late November 1894,
and the "mediumistic astral peregrinations"
of Miss Élise-Catherine Müller of Martigny, Switzerland,
(named Hélène in the literature) begin here, and will last

five years. Five years of intricate trances, and their
on-the-scene reports from that neighboring planet.
*Mitchma mitchmon mimini tchouainem mimatchenig
masichinof mezavi tatelki abresinad navette naven navette
mitchiichenid naken chinoutfiche:* "Hélène

herself will speak Martian." In the company of friends
as well as under the scrupulous scrutiny of psychologist
Théodore Flourney, this seemingly ordinary
middle-class silk-shop salesperson undertakes
the episodes of what becomes a startling psychic odyssey
in the annals of "disincarnate travel" (or,
I would also argue, of travel literature of any kind).

Look, the sky is all red . . . a rose-coloured fog. . . .
Quick, please, give me paper!

Of her spoken and written Martianese:
"It is, indeed, a language
and not a simple jargon or gibberish of vocal noises
produced at the hazard of the moment without any stability."
    From out of the fog—he is riding in a miza,
    a "moving house" without wheels or horses—
"It cannot be denied the following characteristics—First:
It is a harmony of clearly articulated sounds,
grouped so as to form words. Secondly:"
    —with a beast, a "pet," with the "head of a cabbage"
    and one great eye in the middle, like a peacock feather
    that moves on paws—
"These words when pronounced express definite ideas.
Thirdly, and finally:"
    and aquatic creatures, they look like giant snails
    —meanwhile, Astané has a grotto for meditation
    carved out of the mountainside
"Connection of the words with the ideas is continuous; or,
to put it differently, the signification of the Martian terms
is permanent and is maintained
from one end to the other of the texts which have been collected
in the course of now three years."
    —and a hall of infants set on yellow moss;
    and there are animals, almost hairless,
    and with the large soft eyes of seals—and these
    have tubes attached to their udders by the men,
    and these infants are fed on the milk
"It is the complete fabrication of all of the parts of a new language."
    —and I was there.

one red fantastic corpuscle
at the center of her brain,
one red amazing impervious corpuscle,
three inches in;
                three zillion light years

≈

My sister returns from her shit job; phonecalldemeaning
deadlinedemeaning teleconferencedemeaning shit pay.
The kids the dog the evening meal the laundry
the bills the pills to pick up at Drug Rite,
and Dannie—*pecktothecheek*—he'll rise now
from a day of M.S. reverie and greet her.
"He *tries* to help around, but—" (shrug). My sister

isn't the woman I've invented
for the introductory section, she
of the quiet disappointments, who speaks
for so many of us. And maybe my sister here
is only "my sister"—one more fiction;
this isn't meant to be autobiography.
Still, I understand what she's thinking tonight

as she stares in the mirror and dabs
the day's mascara with her cleansing pad:
this isn't the life she'd planned on having
(that commonest of American misgivings).
It may be strengthened by the invisible struts of love
in any number of viable ways, and yet . . .
this isn't where she thought she'd arrive.

My brother-in-law on the living-room sofa.
My brother-in-law how many mental-states-of-himself
removed from the living-room sofa?
how many alternate Dannies, alternate
chronologies and galaxies, does he get to explore in exchange
for being unable to press
the gas and brake in the Honda?
Question: how far could you fall if you fell
like energy into a microchip?

And how far has my sister come
to stand at this bathroom mirror
in its unconcealing light?
There is no standard unit of measurement for this,
but I think /she looks, and looks/
the face can be an odometer.

3.

And he will describe for you these numerous wonders,
of Lands and divers Peoples, and of heathenish Customs,
also of the Creatures of these places.
—Marco Polo. Ah, yes:
". . . a hidden city as profligately topped
with golden domes as a bakery table might be with dollops
of eclair cream." ". . . an ascension of mist
that begins at the foot of the waterfall, so vast it seems
as if an entire town were created of vapor."
/*numerous wonders*/ It's a craving for this gawk-response
in the face of the sheerly amazing, it's
this goosebumps of the retina, of the breath,
that kickstarts most of us out of our sedimentary slew
and sends us posing for those Ms. (or Mr.) Zombie
passport photos. Surely we want to think of wonder
as Parnassuslike in scale—*a parade*
before the Empress of a thousand temple dancers
on a thousand temple elephants—but
just as surely it can be a single life
in size; on the lonely tableland of northern Tibet,
explorer Alexandra David-Neel sees a distant moving dot:
a *lung-gom-pa,* a lama whose mystic way
is "wonderful endurance," is a "tramping
. . . without stopping during several successive days and nights"
across that normally empty limitlessness.
The lama (in a trance; that is, "with the god in him")
approaches, closer; she writes, "The man did not run.
He seemed to lift himself from the ground,
proceeding by leaps with the elasticity of a ball.
The right hand held a *phurba* (magic dagger)
and moved slightly at each step as if leaning on a stick,
just as though the *phurba,* whose pointed extremity
was far above the ground, had touched it
and were actually a support." At which
description, a wild frisson of awe shoots through me.
—*Not* the reigning sensibility
                              in the letters
of Thomas Gray. In 1739 he travels from Great Britain
to the Continent: "There are Trees, & Houses
just as in England." And writes of himself, laconically,
"Goes into the Country to Rheims in Champagne.

Stays there 3 Months, what he did there
(he must beg the reader's pardon, but)
he has really forgot."
                          Some do best
rooted. (Gray, for instance,
back again in London, gives posterity his grandly visioned,
vastly moralizing *Elegy Written in a Country Churchyard*
—"The paths of glory lead but to the grave," etc.).
Dickinson made a circuit of Einstein's universe every day
in her garden in Amherst. And this barnacle
on a wheelchair, its fourth-dimensional mind out touring
post-Einsteinian hyperspace . . . ?—is
Stephen Hawking, stationary lama of the millennium.
His travel is into the endless viridian-manganese sea
of phosphenes in the eye, and then through it,
and into the subumbilicus of Everything and Nothing,
of the proto-breath of the proto-word
of the cosmic Open Sesame.
                          That's a looooong way

∾

from the level at which the contrapuntal rhythm of things
for most of us gets played out. In this city
this morning, the dawn sun glints pristinely
off the clean lines of a building where the blueprints
of the cyberzip electrotechno future are created
out of silicon and wish. And in the shadow of this building,
not a two-block walk away, the Middle Ages is finishing
one more piss-pants night. You can tell
by the burnt cat on the hood of a truck, and by the zonked-out
teenie hooker sweetly singing glory hallelujah
through her caked puke, you can tell
by the ten billion eyes of a plague as it waits for its chance
on a needletip, and by these guys who are whipping each other
drunkenly with ripped-out car antennas,
and by the stabs of love, and by the love of stabbing,
you can tell that as the supersonic cruiser
slips across the sky, it passes for a heartbeat blur
above the year 1000,

where we still live,
in an everpast.

grafitto
in the courthouse john:
goin nowhere
fast

finish

"On 27 February 1914, shortly after midday,
we started down the River of Doubt
into the unknown."
                        —While Theodore Roosevelt explored this
sprig of the Amazon, and Alexandra David-Neel
entered Lhasa disguised as a Tibetan beggar woman
(1914 too) and Sir Aurel Stein discovered the Cave
of the Thousand Buddhas (1907) and Robert Edwin Peary
arrived at the North Pole (1909) in a flurry
"of dogs, sledges, ice, and cold"
                        —Claude Monet
was painting, and had been painting, and would continue
faithfully painting, water lilies and light
in his garden at Giverny. You can see
by the way the petals are as indefinite as flame,
and by the way their watery filaments seem to drill
so deep they suckle on a broth at the heart of the world,
what a lifetime pilgrimage this was
for him, though not one
of mobility.
                        While I think
of his haystacks series I first saw when I was seven
at the Chicago Art Institute (1955)—and
how these great lumps move
from being on fire at sunbreak,
through the color-chart declensions of the light,
to their late-in-the-day reserve,
gravid with plum and indigo—
                        Monet is leaning,
stick-man that he is by now, on the rail of a bridge
across his lily pond, and thinking
backward into time, to a confluence of many
earlier waters:
                        Venice, Amsterdam,
the dazzling chop of the Seine, and ocean water churning
into white carnations on the sand. . . .
And at this point, our introductory-section woman
enters the poem again, returned to us
over so much time like an object
lost in the sea, and then suddenly washed to shore,
back into the light we live by.

Without ever speaking to us, or reading these words,
she thinks it too: that she's been lost
for years in mysterious travel,
turned in its current, worked
a molecule at a time by this.
And now she's beach glass—now she's something
beautiful but reduced.
Yes, that's it: beach glass.
With her soft hues.
With her awkward, glossy finish.

trouble, with pleasant interludes

Against

In the medieval village, "decisions respecting plowing,
planting, weeding, harvesting, pasturing,"
were based upon community consent: the entire
adult population was a part of this agreement.
Or think of nation-states eventually coming to terms
beneath a truce flag. But in the Center
for Marital Counsel today, these two
refuse agreement on the budgie's plastic water dish,
on a sprinkle of salt, on a nose hair, on a nail head.
There's something almost admirable
in the obdurate integrity, the *purity,* they bring
to what would otherwise be petty spite.
They won't agree on a button-snap, on a postage stamp,
they couldn't on the same day both say *yes* to the same coriander seed.

∾

T's father, eighty-one, was only shut in what the children called
"the care home" by a week before a tumor-laden X ray
of his wife's meant that the children swiftly placed her
in that euphemistic, wretched place as well. Now
they were roommates, after sixty years of marriage.
And you'd think that, in the disinfected shadow
Death casts there, they'd ease their sixty years
of differences, of bickering, with a front of united defiance.
Ha. "It's TOO WARM, do the thermostat." "Don't
TOUCH it! It's CHILLY in here." "Yeah, in your head
it's chilly." Maybe it *is* defiance,
is the flag most drenched in the spitfire raging of life
that they can yet wave. They become a salient lesson:
We will go to our graves contending.

∾

I was seventeen, and making goofy googoo talk
to Lyla Rolker, sixteen, who was miles of untouched whipping cream
and a beaconlike dollop of civet musk and several feet
of artfully batted eyelash. That's when Nate Yblonsky,
eighteen years and 218 pounds of football practice, sidled up
and taught me something intense about the idea
of territoriality. Ah, the always powerful I/Thou, Me/World
interface! In medieval villages every spring,
the village boundaries were recommitted to memory
in a walk around the perimeter called "a-ganging."
And to emphasize this lore for them, they'd dunk
small boys in boundary brooks, and knock them
into especially important configurations of boundary rocks,
and smack their silly heads against the trees.

There, Too

I'm not the dapper man in the lambswool overcoat.
I'm not the woman unfolding the mail, lost
in a lozenge of light by the vase of roses and ferns.
I'm not the man with the cocky swagger
and fresh dirt under his fingernails.
I'm the triangle—that's right, I'm the triangle

that they make, the way it's made every day
in movies and cheapie self-destructo novels:
steamily, greasily, and I protest this
smutting of my self. I was there

with the square and the circle, originally,
when shape was something pure
and transcendental—long before
the borders-smudging confusion of human affairs.

Whenever you're with another person
—even with who you think of
as *the* other person—I tell you

that the mind and the heart are too bountiful for fidelity,
and I'm there, too.

Ancestored-Back *Is the Overpresiding Spirit of This Poem*

If only somebody would drill with a finger-long rig down
into my skull, and saw a tiny circle out of its bone,
so pools of acid antsiness and angst can steam away;
so all of the great in-gnarling, all of the bunched-up
broodiness can breathe; and so at least the day's
accumulated ephemera, its fenderbender squabbles,
its parade of petty heartache can evaporate in writhes
of sour mist—this spatting couple, for example,
in the booth across the aisle as I'm chowing on a burger
and their every more-than-whispered perturbation is,
this afternoon, a further furrow worked into my mind. . . .
You know I'm kvetching metaphorically. But literalist
Amanda Fielding, wielding a scalpel and electric drill,
bored a hole in her skull in 1970, filming that self-surgery,

∾

and zealously thereafter promoting the benefits of this
third eye, finally "running for Parliament on a platform
of trepanation for national health." The operation
was successfully conducted in the Stone Age (72 %
of the skulls we've found reveal that the patients far survived
that crisis moment), and the Chinese medico Thai Tshang Kung
(150 B.C.) was said "to cut open the skulls of the sick
and arrange their brains in order." A Roman physician's
effects from the second century A.D. include a trepanation kit
in bronze, its tooth-edged bit and driving-bow
as finely produced as any machine-tooled apparatus
a surgeon in 1996 would wish for—when the bow unfolds
it's as intricate in its simplicity as a line of true haiku.
I've read a book whose major pleasure is its breathlessness

∾

in gasping at the ancientness of various devices,
flushing toilets(!) condoms(!) hand grenades(!)—the book
is a grove of invisible exclamation points. These
green glass beads like rain-splats on a leaf
—4,000 years ago. Bone dice, the same. The ribbed vault
in this early Gothic church is a masterly hollowing-out
of space—but houses of *literal* ribs, of mammoth bones,
were sturdy dwellings 15,000 years ago. Rhinoplasty(!)
soccer(!) odometers(!) "Butter" (a favorite sentence)
"spread everywhere, once it was discovered." Though we don't know
poot about the urgent stirrings in our own hearts
or the dreams irrupting nightly in our own heads,
we've been diagramming stars on plaques
of tortoise plate and antler, we've made sky maps,

≈

from before we even understood the link of sex
to birth. And if our coin-op slot machines
can be ancestored-back to that Greco-Egyptian
contrivance of Heron of Alexandria (by which
a dropped-in-place five-drachma bronze piece
starts the portioned flow of a worshiper's ablution-water) . . .
if *ancestored-back* is the overpresiding spirit
of this poem . . . we *are* the progeny of stars,
we *are* their original core-born elements
in new recombination, densed and sizzled into
sentience and soul. I can't imagine the interior tumult
driving Amanda Fielding and her followers, but
I'm not surprised our smallest human units were created
in explosion, speed, and void. My friends

≈

are not the kind to drill their heads and rid themselves
of troubles by decanting. Even so, I've seen them consider
their restless faces in the mirror and wish for *some* release.
Our daily dole of woe is unrelenting. In this burger joint,
in the Booth of a Thousand Sorrows across the aisle,
they're arguing still. Outside, the snow provides each tree
with a clerical collar—this couple is arguing. Outside,
the setting summer sun makes each tree a flambeau
—this couple is arguing, they'll never stop, their joys
have been prodigious and their anti-joy will balance this
or more, the hands with which they make their hard points
in the air are hands of oxygen and nitrogen and argon
older than dust or salt. It's midnight. How
emphatic we can be. How long they've been at it.

Imps

Fire isn't allowed, for the sake of the books.
The lean monk-copyist who scribes the books is slate-blue at his fingertips
this steely late-November day in the year 1000. Brother Ambrosio
huffs some perfunctory warmth on his stiffening hands,
then bends again to his goat's-horn of ink. For every line,
he believes, he's forgiven a sin. And now he's at his heavy
uncial letters, and will be for nine hours more,
until a slab of bread and a beet relieve his transcriptual ardor.
What he copies?—psalter, missal, hagiography:
the predetermined and sanctioned community passions
of a religious culture. Nothing like the twentieth century's
prevalent kneejerk "self-expression." Nothing like the priest,

excuse me: *former* priest, and former nun, on daytime talk TV,
who live, she tells us, in a "trinity of love" with the former
creator-of-tourist-ashtrays-out-of-catfish-heads. This is,
she insists, the final and jubilant stage of a lifelong "quest
to feel belongingness" initiated thirty years before
by parents skittering cross-country with the military: *they*
were wholly rootless, and so *she* grew up "unable to commit." The following day,
a man confesses to pedophilia because of a lesbian aunt.
A woman says she robbed the Sack-N-Save of $13.42
"because of what they're dumping in the water supply, it makes me
go all freaky." Steve was bounced out from The Chicken Shack
"because I'm Scandinavian." The culture

of blame is *so* completely exterior in its search for cause,
some days I wake to think I'll find most people laboring
under the weight of sci-fi-style mind parasites, like fleshy turbans
spewing in, and feeding off, their brain blood. This (by "this"
I mean of course a recognition of the magic of objective correlative
boppin' about in the spotlight) is, to some length,
understandable: you can't beat the miniscule carry-along
convenience of a silicon chip invisibly set in something,
BUT for sheer persuasive visual power, *that* can't touch
a 1940s generating plant, its giant Alcatrazian shape
against the sky, and the enormous wrestling electrical crackles
snaking its rooftop pylon. In the scriptorium, even

—such an isolated unit of human endeavor, its limited range
of reactions surely is pure—when Brother Ambrosio
nods off, sleepy in his long day's long eighth hour
of thickly nibbed and careful letters, he knows
it's imps in league with Satan that keep pulling down his eyelids.
If in scratching his flea-measled thigh he spills
a hand's-expanse of ink across the vellum page, the fleas
are tiny devils on a guerilla mission from Hell.
And once a devilkin took lodging in his belly, and there
created "rumbling noises like a toad, and which, for hours,
spoiled the concentration of all of the other Brothers."
We find parchment scraps with appropriate exorcisms:

"Away! you flaming sow, you poisoned udder,
you arse of the arch-fiend, shit-fly, stinking he-goat,
out out out, away, back into thine infernal kitchen,
you bestial puke!" We also find
those charming marginal doodles (sprigs in flower,
unicorns, seemingly every songbird in Creation): such
diminutive external bodies given to the longings of these
cooped-up men. And when they came to drag my friend Jess
screaming to the ward, because he was beating his head
on the lawyer's steps, it was clear to us all that the chemicals
in his mind had turned against him. It was clear to Jess
that he was being hunted like prey by hounds from the moon.

The Number of Utterly Alien Civilizations in Star Trek *and* Star Wars

He *likes* to be touched—it must be
it reminds him of his mother's nightly
fussy tuck, her brush-of-his-cheek,
and all of the other subsequent formative contact
from the world: the jockly high-fives in the gym,
an early girlfriend's sweetly puckered smacks
along his inner thighs . . . as if his life has licked him

into hale shape, from out of no-shape,
like a dam bear overseeing its cub. Then
he weds. And *she?*—well, let's say
that her childhood is a series of sudden
physical encounters best left undetailed here.
From these apart approaches, we can predicate
endless scenarios, but I don't mean marriage

only. For example, on Christmas Eve in 1100,
the Lord of the Manor of Upper Gooseholm
adjusted his rabbit-and-squirrel-trimmed tunic
about his girth, and at a table lit at either end
by silver candelabra, sat to a dinner of calf brain,
flank of deer, roast wood duck, honeyed ale,
and upland eels simmered in buttery ewes' milk; while

the annual treat bestowed upon his villagers
was breadsops and a slice per house of baconfat,
most likely shared with the rats that lived in the thatching
—a distance of style as psychologically vast across
as is the Great Red Spot of Jupiter ("three Earths could fit
inside it"), astronomically. When archeologists
spaded up the artifacts of Gooseholm,

they discovered a Roman outpost under those
and, under *that,* the stony hints
of an Early Bronze Age settlement still in place,
still meaning a time and a people, as if
the later layers above—straight up to Crazy Maisie's
Super Pizza & Video Shack—
were only so much weather. There's no such thing

as one planet. It's all science fiction.
It's all a billion planets.

"Of Course *They're Strangers. They* Aren't Me."

I'll tell you about "the Major" three doors south of here,
he fashions birds of candle wax—sparrows, jays—exactly
duplicated around a complicated copper-wire armature,
and then he convincingly jackets them in feathers from actual
dead birds that we find it especially convenient not
to ask about. At Donut Diner, the Widow Sloane
will dolefully inform you of "the button" in her left
(or right: it varies) ear, through which "the masters"
speak and make her shudder so, that once she wet
her good pants in the taxi. And I'll tell you, too:

I've made them up, to represent your officemate
you interrupted yesterday in going back to grab an extra folder,
who was whipping at his bad left thigh
with a strap in his Mother Superior of a left hand,
who was whimpering, who represents the woman
at the bus stop with a past she drags behind her
like a conga line of corpses, and she'll share with you
the name of each, and the special handmade sorrow of each,
and how the particular worm in the heart of each one
burrows into hers. As if she's saying: *you'll* understand.

≈

Where do we come from, out of what smouldering crevice
in our brainstems do we crawl, to bear
such furred or scaled lumps to one another?
—like coal miners, only
self miners. Only spelunkers,
only bathysphere explorers,
of the psychological lamb's-foot jelly
shivering at the core of the id. But all that's
metaphorical, like the pool balls we see
atoms as. Where *do* we come from? Kansas

countryside won't hold the eye. You're always aware
of the sky heaped heavily over it, past air, past where
the o's of *ozone* empty into that sweep of void
and scattered pinpoint fire we call the empyrean.
I've idled on the clay and gravel roads that sprig these fields,
watching distant towns so drowned below the heavens,
so beneath a comprehension, they were relics
in a kind of archeology no one's invented yet.
It's like—we come into one another's lives
from Atlantis, we rise from so deep.

∾

Native of India, Fred spoke singing Americanese
in that beautiful bird-inflected flutter
they never lose. He told me about his work
on the Browning collection, and the stiffly formal details of his visit
to the Queen Mother, to note the Browning Jubilee.
"Not bad," with a wink, "for someone who isn't Christian,
Buddhist, or Mohammedan." So I made the obvious
joke, and extended my hand for a shake: "A fellow Jew!"
"Oh no," he corrected me very
very seriously; I was speaking with the only

practicing orthodox Zoroastrian in Kansas.
"Ahura Mazda is The One True God. You would like to see
my undergarment?" This, in the third-floor offices
of Kansas Book Recycling, over Lin Foo Chinese Carryout,
next to the Greyhound station. Fred continued
processing used textbooks as he talked at me.
"And when I die, they will set my body atop
the Tower of Silence"—now his eyes took on a dreamy light,
as if he were describing the glowingest heaven—
"and vultures will pick my bones clean!"

Complete with Starry Night and Bourbon Shots

Morgan's father will be mailed to her,
they've said in a letter—now that every bequested
dole of his body has been banked away,
the residue in its factory urn will be mailed.
She says Stephanie sometimes wiggles her fingers around
inside *her* father, so the bone chips
clink against the fired clay, and I suggest
the final char of Bob Potts be sealed inside maracas;
"He'd like that," Morgan says, especially if the Texas
Sexoramas used him percussively, his favorite
country-funk group. What she'll really do
this June is scatter him into the air
of Mount Palomar, "because he loved his telescope." Let him
circle and settle, circle, circle, and settle.

≈

He also loved his drink, but nó one mentions
touring the Pearl Beer plant and surreptitiously adding him
to a vat. The stories are legion,
legend: for instance Bill English of English's Bar
in one clean squeeze deadeyeing a shot glass
off his pate. Though now that's decades gone.
When I met him even his *teeth* were grizzled
—up at the bar surrounded by all of the gleaming
palomino hotpants twenty-year-olds of Austin, Texas;
reading Kipling's *Kim* in the sonic boomboom rock.
I first ate pit-cooked cabrito at one of his parties,
lank and sharp and good. Then doing our names
on the lawn, from the bones—in the light,
and in the easiness, before anything like that seemed symbolic.

≈

The Wild West–style saloon doors of "The Hall of Horns"
(the brewery's tourist annex) open grandly on its choice, thematic
gawkables: a map of the United States entirely
done from snake rattles; sturdy desks, and chairs, and armoires
completely or near-completely from antlers and hooves.
Also the monstrosities: the Siamese-twin calves
with braided horns, like a Swedish Christmas candle;
the calf with horns that horribly loop forward and enter
its eye sockets. Yes, and there were those Victorian museums
of human residue: the brains of criminals floating like compote,
the gold-cased tibias and jaws of saints. Our wonderment
can seize on something commoner than these, without
diminishing: a skeleton of an owl, and the ribs of its digested
field mouse suddenly tumbling out.

～

Because he loved his telescope . . . he's being flung under
everything above, the whole night sky is called upon
to be his memorial marker. Maybe our obligation
is finding lines from star to star up there:
the new bones of his new, if metaphysical,
existence. Etc., etc.—sky and bones, the stuff
of sonnets. Some people like calling the heavens
star-complected, to some that's "precious" odium. Tastes
differ. *My* father was heavily lowered into the earth,
is earth by now, is the dry click of ants in the grasses.
Still, I think that they might meet at the horizonline,
Bob Potts and my father. Maybe they're having a metaphysical
quaff right now, remembering how one's son and one's daughter
divorced each other—one of the copious little deaths.

～

Even microscopic radiolarians have skeletons, and this
alone can jolt our cogitation meters into the red
astonishment zone—what then to make of Morgan's parcel
flying through the mail? Not that comedy, say, or bereavement
are matters of size. And still it's the whale I think of,
washed ashore in 1564 on Nod Thwaite's property:
yes, the whale would do, as a unit for Morgan to measure by.
Thwaite cleaned each stave, and on a brisking autumn day
when his buffing was done, began to charge admission to that osseous
parthenon. Hundreds took the tour. By night a fire
threw the vaulting into flickery relief. By day they clambered
their midget way among these ruins. I like them mostly
in the skull; as if a whale were dreaming of what it had been
before it turned from that and chose the sea.

◦∾

I'm sorry, but this gray vase bearing gray debris,
this poof and its stringbean pieces of bone, is no
Bob Potts in his cardigan flecked with pipe shag
holding court at The Cedar Door or Mulligan's.
No. This vase is Nothing; its contents, Nothing.
And Nothing can't be counterbalanced. I'm sorry,
there isn't a fact that can do it, there isn't
a richly glitzed-up fiction in the world, not God,
not no-God, there isn't a memory that means anything
to Nothing. And Morgan says, with a tender shake of her head,
"That man," as if he might have been some feathercrested
platinum-shitting prodigy, "was something."
Even without his eyes he was something, without
his legs, and in the final sour bubble of breathing: something.

◦∾

Because he loved his telescope . . . he's given away
to that emptiness now, he's sprinkled from a daughter's fingers
into the galaxy pinch by pinch. As physics knows,
and so as endless poems these days repeat, we're all
constructed of the particles of stars. The service
may as well go *dust to dust, and astra to astra.*
Not that any rhetoric really comforts.
Not that any glint of wit or thundered scripture
suffices for long. But since you've asked for a poem,
my ex, my sweet and troubled one, I'll give you this
attempt, complete with starry night and bourbon shots:
Here,
I'm lifting a beer
for Bob Potts.

In

the text:
& then the author's life

behind the text:
& then the preexisting

psychic fundament behind *that:*
always further layers penetrable

or not:
the word & its origin

& its intention
& its several dozen possible meanings

in several dozen heads:
not to mention the moment

& the moment before:
not to mention let's say love

& then the word "love"-(a)
that's painted over with "love"-(b)

very impasto
very very impasto: always text

& overtext: always
&eavertext

~

He hiked the strenuous trails—and above.
He did the Stätzerhorn (8,593 feet)
and the Lenzerhorn (9,703) and the Piz Bernina
(13,284). There would be storms at times
—the ice axe and the crampons little help in this
opacity, as Alpine snow *became* the air—but mostly
it was the clarity of vision at these supernal heights
that lifted him like a pocket's lining
out of himself; and he could see
the glitter of a river in some distant glacial valley,
every pock of a boulder along its twists
as obvious as the alpenroses and edelweiss beside his booted feet.
—The way (and now he remembers) that he was ten and leaning
observantly over the lucid waters of the Grift, and staring
straight to the river's utterly evident bottom muck: the feeling
was that he could peel that dirt back now
and stare with a similar potency at
the living chthonic heart of the world. . . . Remembering this.
Wilhelm Röntgen. November 1895: what should he call this
ray that he's discovered, this mystery force, this X.

∾

This is how we fought: we rubbed the skin off
one another's minds. Because we were married,
because we'd learned through intimacy
the weak link and the likeliest archeology-point
for quick unearthing, this is how we did it:
we worried the top skin off the mind, and then
the underskin, we reached inside with eyes that saw
through history, and lifted from out of each other
the oiliest, inch-squirm maggot-thing-of-an-idea
we could find in the gnarls, and held it
to the light. It was on one of those days
I thought back to the fluoroscopes so popular
for viewing the fit of kids' shoes in the early 1950s.
I was . . . five, I'd guess. Across the store, a girl of five
was ushered in a pair of deeply lacquer-looking party shoes
to the huge machine, for her regiment of bones to be put
on parade for the world—her inside life, her own.
I'd never seen such frightful screaming. "Albert,
you're not a baby like *that.*" Oh, maybe; maybe not.
I know I understood her shock at that radiatory undoing.

∾

When you invoke the grand metonymy,
when you ask for a hand in marriage . . .

                       oh

it will stroke you, gently/sexually;
it will hammer your back, a ballpeen fist;
and often it will be one part of the shrug
that says our every attempt to fashion something
shared between two people is laced with a basic
unreadability . . .

                   he was silent,
as if he had left his mind in the laboratory. . . .
He picked at his food without enjoyment. . . .
She began to worry. . . . She asked. . . .
He made no reply . . . apparently had angered him. . . .
He disappeared through the open door,
walked along the hallway and entered his study. . . .
She went to bed alone, leaving him in the laboratory. . . .
(W. Robert Nitske, in *The Life of Wilhelm Conrad Röntgen*).
Evening: December 22, 1895:

                   "Bertha, may I have /

                    ~

. . . her hand / in its consent / her hand
in all of its physical "hereness," yes, but also
in all of its new "new physics" insubstantiality /
holding still for fifteen minutes on the plate /
amid the induction coils and pear-shaped Hittorf-Crookes tubes
and the Lenard tubes and Ruhmkorff coil and Raps pump /
here: her hand: her famous hand: the famous fingerbones
showing up with the jointing and elegant length
of bamboo done in a gray wash: here: her fingerbones
like the legs of the deep-sea spider crab /
the famous photographed enterable flesh /
and the famous two resistant rings:
those dark and obdurate things:
as if all of the hesitant pleasures
and go-for-broke hell-bent inanities
and desecrations and choked-down hopes and heavings
of a marriage
here were locked to the bone
in mineral form so concentrated, nothing, *nothing,*
could light their essential privacy.

∽

there's an airplane in this poem
that won't go away, it circles

insistently, is shooed off
but returns, is here like a fly

in the room in 1995
as the two of us bicker and icily stare,

and is there in 1895 somehow
before its invention at Kitty Hawk,

it's in the thin blue winter air
as Röntgen walks with Bertha

in their fur coats
to the mailbox on the Pleicherring

with copies of his initial report,
it snaps them

and it listens in,
its lenses and its microphones

are overhead, relentless
in the way that the author and reader are

as the characters step to the therapist's all-ears couch,
as the characters start to strip

≈

. . . and the bones in his wife's hand. No doubt it was this last capability that
made Röntgen's discovery the first modern scientific breakthrough to spark
banner headlines in newspapers around the world. Some anxious people even
began taking baths fully clothed, convinced that scientists were lurking about
their houses peering at them with these mystery rays.
   —Marcia Bartusiak

She wants, she says, "more sharing" in this
relationship, more swappage of our days' individual freight.
Okay. What *I've* been doing is reading
about the application of Röntgen's uncorked power.
In 1925, forensic detective Edward Oscar Heinrich had
"the corpse sent to his laboratory and X-rayed.
He immediately observed that a molar was missing,"
and, soon enough: case closed! It's similarly handy
when a jewel thief's nabbed in flight and slyly swallows
the incriminating diamond. Maybe my favorite
tale is someone stopped when airport security sees
the X-rayed shape of a gun in her carry-on; and
she pleads with increasing intensity as they open her bag
for the snooping world to wonder at
her steel-cored dildo-*cum*-balls. —And how
was *your* day, where have you been? At that,
my wife's face storms protectively
around some inmost selfhood of the night, and this
gets ranted: You/can/NOT/know-
EV/'ry/SIN/gle/thing/that/hap/pens/in/MY/MIND!

≈

. . . And I watch her sleep. I study her in sleep
until I'm hypnotized, and think that I can see
our trouble feeding on the reeds inside her (even as its sister
swims in me), a bloated, scales-covered thing with fearsome
beauty of its own. In the book of "radiological photographs
of nature," every leaf of chard and every balled-up grub
becomes a reliquary rayed to reveal
extraordinary interiorscapes: a minaret,
in a water lily; the swaddled hooded-cobra-head of the clitoris,
in a cowrie shell; my grandmother's sinuous intricate
hook-and-eyelet leather strips along her orthopedic boots,
in the length of the rat snake. . . . Strangeness,
loveliness. In Röntgen's early study of a custodian,
the clothes and then the flesh have drizzled transparently
away and leave the metal keys on either hip
like a schoolboy's catch of minnows after a day at the stream.
We all have fish in our chests. We all have
rings of keys, and knots of barbed wire, and jellyfish stingers,
and overblown roses, and shake our sediments up
and we all contain an undulant wing of lees.

≈

When I watched them wheel my father into the lab
(I wasn't used to—then—a hospital's visual rigamarole),
what struck me hardest wasn't the vividly purple-green
tarantula the needle bruised into his skin;
or the dolly the bag rode on, that accompanied him
like a gaunt and silent retainer; or even the catheter tube
that seemed as thick as an eel set to drink his pee . . . no:
No, it was the G-string—except, about the size of home plate—
made of lead, that they hung at his crotch
as they placed him inside what looked like a toll-guard booth.

The booth's front side is glass: the "private dancer"
faces out, then there's an immediate akimbo
display of the goods. Some dancers obviously resent
their work, and some take powerful pleasure from
its muff-and-money mix. But *this* never varies:
"Where are you from?" "Connecticut," she says
(she's from Montana). Former job? "Uh—waitress"
(a courier for Trans-Send). Kids? "Yeh, two of them" (no).
It's her lead shield. There are places
even your goddam hard-earned dollar won't let you go.

≈

He was meticulous, and cautious; when the badgerers
from the newspapers all demanded he prognosticate some marvelous
applications of his discovery, he demurred: "I am not
a prophet, and I am opposed to prophesying"; it wasn't
marvels that he sought, but what was
measurably there. His world was one of verification
won in small and graphable increments. And yet
with Bertha gone—she died October 31 in 1919—
sometimes he read aloud from the newspaper
or a novel they had liked, or mail received, pretending
that she still shared her thoughts with him.
(Whitman has this two-line poem from his old age:
"These carols sung to cheer my passage through the world I see,
For a completion I dedicate to the Invisible World."
I think of Röntgen completing himself that way.)
And so this is where we should leave him, yes?
—Sitting there,
           rocking,
                   intimately speaking
into the gateway of X.

∾

Sentences have a noun phrase as the subject followed by a verb phrase as the predicate. That rule is needed to account for such sentences as The woman wept. *Note that* The gun wept *also follows this rule, but it is not an acceptable sentence.*
  —George A. Miller, in *The Science of Words*

Under the rubble of World War II is the rubble of World War I.
And under that is a layer of struggle-to-make-ends-meet
and yet bucolic, warless village-and-shepherding life. And
under that, intact, is a circle of dwellings structured
out of tusks and reinforced mud. And under that, some
bones—like accent marks distributed in the Earth—
including some earliest human skulls. And in them:
tiny figures, each with tiny skulls of their own,
and brains the size of garden snails' bodies that,
like any brains, are larger than the universe that holds them.
Out of yours, we took a hatchet that mewed my name;
and out of mine, we took a perfectly innocent-looking freestone peach
that was a grenade. So easy—once the monstrous pain
from sawing the skull-tops off was numbed. And we arranged it
all on the table: the gun that wept, the tear that burnt
like a spill at the foundry, a clock of teeth
and sexual lubrication, an open sore that winked
just like a flirting eye, a lightless sun, a pastry made of pins.
And we said: Here is the marriage, I hate you,
here is the marriage, heal it, heal it.

∼

There's an airplane in the skies, from somewhere
out of poetic eternitime, it hides

between the couplets, it disguises its noise
in the general human buzz, it lands

some pages back, in the Alps, and deposits
a microsurveillance device in one of those alpenroses

you read about. Yes, you
—you're being watched. We know all about you.

As a compensation, of course, you get to voyeurize
this couple in their most distressed extremes;

although another way of saying them right now
would be this tender evocation Rembrandt has done

of a woman in difficult contemplation, as she sits
on the rim of her bath. X-ray analysis

shows an earlier composition
under the current surface, shows us really

another woman inside this woman.
It's late afternoon; the day folds up.

Another head is in her head,
and wearily rests against it.

more trouble with pleasant interludes

Squash and Stone

Like so many men of his time, he was after a grand principle that would explain
a universal truth. An element that he called "septon" was, he declared, the instru-
ment of decay and the cause of most diseases. He lectured on septon, wrote papers
on it and even composed a long poem called "The Doctrine of Septon," in which
his doggerel blamed septon for cancer, leprosy, scurvy and ringworm.
   —on the nineteenth-century naturalist Samuel Latham Mitchill, collaged
     from Joseph Kastner's *A Species of Eternity*

And so it is, with the physicists' need
to find a simple, nonexclusionary Supertheory that gathers
the "weak," "strong," gravitational, and electromagnetic
forces into a single "field." And so it was with the marriage.
We wanted its failures in a single word
that ends in -ism or -phobia. One thumb to suck.
One wilted plant to mourn for or renurture.
Isn't it difficult enough, to be a "me" in a world
of daily half-price sales at the Chooz-a-Self?
We wanted the flaw in "us" to be a single, lucid wrongness
(that would require a single righting).
Of course we wanted this; the Supertheory is meant to be
completion raised to beauty,
the way the ocean is both the ocean and the sky.
I'd see her sitting in the kitchen some days staring
at a random still-life basketful of leeks and summer squash
as if this might comprise a read-out screen, a Ouija mechanism,
to the planet of The Single Reason. Once, she said,
she watched me in the dusk light try to squeeze a stone,
she said I really looked as if . . . she thought
of a film noir private detective trying to make a suspect talk.
I remember a day when the mill across the county line
in Nestorville caught fire, and I wished the arm of char
it raised across the sky
would write some Answer, something brief
the way the elementary is by definition brief, and irreducible.
Give us our god, our needle.
Give us our theory, we thought to ourselves,
as if it were a Constitutional right. Give us our septon.

Dog, Fish, Shoes (or Beans)

"I was a shmooshled little girl," my Aunt Elena says.
"I'm seventeen, I have a shape from a matzoh ball,
boomp boomp boomp I walk. So no wonder, Glicka
with big soft eyes like stewed prunes
has a boyfriend, he would jump through hoops of fire
for her if his wizzle was dipped in kerosene first,
and Pearl has a boyfriend, Misha does, Rebekka
whose body goes in and out like an accordion, hooy
she could walk down the street and the trolleys
fall out of their tracks. But poor Elena, me,
boohoo boohoo with the tears all shpritzing, don't
laugh from my story, it's very sad. So what
does Elena do on Saturday night, with everybody else
in front of the radio holding hands to ukelele songs?
Elena, the poor shmo, baby-sits for people
in her building. On the third floor are the Morrises,
with a dog a cocker spaniel—like a bowling ball
of dirty fur and always yapping, I
hated it—and a goldfish. And so for *them*
I don't even *baby*-sit, they would hire somebody
I swear to wipe the dog's tush if they could.
So I stay up there, I feed the fish and the dog,
I clean the box, I listen like an idiot
to the ukelele serenades like everyone else, and I cry.
Good; so this is my Saturday date. One night,
does it *rain?*—like Noah's Flood of a rain.
From nowhere, a Noah's Flood all of a sudden.
I run to close the bedroom window—*whoops,*
and down the three floors goes the goldfish bowl
with Miss Goldilox, which the name is a joke,
like lox the fish, but a goldfish. It lands
in a puddle. I think to myself, 'In a puddle?
Could beeeee . . . this little fishy's heart still beats.' So I

run downstairs—" "—*But,*" my Uncle Mo
takes over, "she leaves the door to the apartment open.
This Is Important: remember. Meanwhile,
a certain very handsome young man—" "—oh, handsome
like a *blintz* that got run over—" "—is delivering
a wagon of shoes from the Jewish Poor Relief Fund—"
"—shoes? it was canned goods—" "—listen
in *your* story maybe it's canned goods, *mine* it's shoes—"
"—okay, Mr. Memory, but I'm telling you I see
these little cans with the pears and the whaddayacallem beans
on the labels—" "—shoes, it was shoes, it was shoes,
up past your winkus in shoes, do you hear me—"
"—don't laugh—" "—so anyway—" "—feh!—" "—where
was I—" "—don't interrupt—" "—and I said
'Pardon me Miss but is this poor shivering
cocker spaniel yours?'—" "—and here we are to tell you
this story Fifty Years Later!" Then we always said:
Did you go upstairs and kiss? And they always
never answered: "The fish, by the way, we never found."
"So you see?" she'd add. "Nothing is hopeless."

In the Bar in the Bar

Someone's voice, made haughtier by her rum-on-ice
than necessary, says "I can see right *through* you," and
I think of that population in the paintings of previous eras
we've subjected to twentieth-century X-ray study:
a world of interior bodies, whole unto themselves,
that are caught torqued contrariwise
to the turn of their outer bodies; of women staring beseechingly
out of the eyes of men—and men, of women—night and night again
at the window; of downswept necks bent in submission
or devotion, like a counterweight
inside the upthrusting faces of prideful defiance . . .
some seem no more than a clever inner puppet show, but others
shriek with the urgency of the prematurely buried. . . . Blurry,
earlier selves. . . . In the oil on panel
Portrait of Edward VI of England, radiography
shows us that the boy-king was a girl once: how
the roundness of her Netherlandish skirt has been
subsumed into his raiment, how her loosely held carnation
has become a tasseled dagger in his grip; how she remains
in him, the living underpinnings he began as. . . . Everybody,
yes?—would seem to be a new home for this old, old cricket
rubbing the ancient music out of its legs. So
when I hear some hombre's slurry bravado
loudly lobbed from a corner (*I fuckin said NO WAY, Miss Kiss-My-Ass*),
I know "this Chinese vessel, a *fang ding,* of the eleventh century B.C.,
shows extensive interior damage under X-ray light,
and clumsy attempts at soldering; a liberal application
of false patina attempts to mask this." When I hear
a woman's martially jolly *OF COURSE I'm happy,*
I TOLD YOU I'm happy, and don't you EVER forget it,
I know "beneath the chest of this tenderly rendered
'infant suckling' set scene, is the breastplate of a warrior
that analysis shows as the painter's original study." Everybody,

yes? In the face in the face. In the bar in the bar.
And it turns out, beer is a kind of crystal ball;
you don't look *into* it, you take it into *you*.
In mine, by midnight, I can read the past
as it rises like mist in front of me. I can read the text
in the text of the wedding. Two of us, saying
eager *yes,* and *yes,* in front of the witnesses. And already,
a head in each of our heads, a mind in each of our minds,
beginning to slowly shake itself
against the thick of the current—*no,* and *no.*

Alternative Uses

*While exploring a branch of the Victoria River, in North Australia, we halted, as
usual, at noon, with scanty rations, which Mr. Gregory improved by taking from
his hat a stout sewing needle, softening it in the fire, and bending it into a fish-
hook, baited with grasshoppers.*
   —nineteenth-century travel account

It will often be found useful to carry a bottle
of cold tea, nothing is so effectual for thirst.
Experienced travellers frequently carry in their holsters,
instead of pistols: in the one, a tiny
teapot with a paper of tea, and in the other,
a cup and a paper of sugar. And in those days
friends would always seem amazed when they suddenly
opened my refrigerator and found—because
I ate my meals in neighborhood cafés and hated to see
good shelf space wasted, and because I wanted
these stacks of nuisance out of sight
as rapidly as my red pen could complete them—
mounds of graded Composition 101 assignments. (And
once, in 103°, a lover's folded lingerie.)

∾

He needed to pretend to be straight, in order
to be promoted; and she had a proven record
of being exactly that, with a skillful ardor.
She needed start-up backing for the catering shop
she dreamed of; and, the heartless bastard,
he'd devoted his life to squeezing money out of others.
He needed a legal reason to stay in the United States,
once his card expired; she needed a father for the baby,
any father. She hated her overrestrictive fundamentalist
parents; he was surely a pile of nasty habits
looking for a container to stain. He
had his agenda, she had hers, and they coincided
along a delicate line. And so they took each other
in holy matrimony.

∾

Hoping this finds you well. There is so little
in the way of news I am almost ashamed to write,
but for the obligation I feel to one who is
himself such a prompt correspondent.
The garden is declaring itself already
this season in butter-yellows and blues that look
as if they want to wave hello all the way
to Turners Crossing and Hill Fork. Oh,
there is a new pastor, sorrily NOT a real rouser
of a sermonizer. Yours, as ever, Imojean T.
The postcard is from 1912, and brittling enough
so that its penny stamp is chipping off, and the spidery
message, hidden under it, says
Hot kisses to my honey boy.

What We're Used To

Or the woman who, after the seeped stink of her death
had slapped the neighbors into attentiveness and then the cops,
was found to have shared the dungeon-dark of her backlot shack
with (this was by actual clicker count) 548 rats, that
(who?) she'd made her confidants—had fed,
and built a gamy junkparts playground for, and nested with
in sleep (perhaps by then could *only* sleep with the familiar
tictac dance of their garbagey paws across her body). And
"familiar" *is* the keynote word: that dankness
was the comfy psyche-soup in which she lazied back
and happily dissolved at the end of a day. For her,
this was natural. In the Hanzai Valley, the villagers

∼

live with ghosts around them as commonly as oxygen
is around them—ghosts, cospatially with the air
they breathe, the air that rides the blood, the air we'll all become
one day, one way or another. "Rounded [cosmos/sky-container]"
(their ritual greeting) they say on meeting any of this invisible
and thronging population. For them, it's natural. The spectral selves
of animals and plants attend the hunt and the fields. Stars,
the various intimacies that occur at night in those fields.
Ancestral spirits see through the dark, of course, and so
not even the fevery knots of the sexual union are secret
from them—if anything, their up-close sidelines cheering
is expected, is part of the order of things. In Rembrandt's

∼

engraving *Het Ledekant,* of a couple in coitus (he's on top
between her legs, in a billowy, canopied four-poster), the woman pictured
in this otherwise realistically rendered bedtime scene is given
three arms; to this extent, the viewer is given two choices.
If we ask to accept the arm that laxly sprawls at her side
(presumably paired with one out of sight, on her other side), then
the woman's nearly asleep, or swoozled on too much wine.
If we ask to accept the hands that clasp his ass in tightly,
the woman's actively passionate: dark lines beneath one hand say
fleshly pressure. Whichever. Neither reading's "wrong." Each
has a naturalness, depending on the lives, and on the thousand
constituent details of their time together. Once I loved

~

in the way I thought love worked: you made
life easier for someone; made it into a calm continuum,
sans burden or suspicion; you were free of frowst and bitterness,
and you trusted that life would buoy you in return. For her,
each day Creation started up from zero again, tough brick by brick,
and debt by debt; attack was ever immanent, defense was ever
hammered-on in thick emotional sheet metal. So it
didn't last. And both of us felt betrayed. I remember . . .
the sun through the bough, like a loading ramp into infinity . . .
I explained my idea of life, and I could see it wasn't material
at all, it was a phantom life, and she could put her hand right through me:
I was supernatural.

The Lost Continent *(1951)*

The purse-snatch in this 1568 painting of Bruegel's
squats behind his victim in a clearly absurdist rendering.
He wears—he's *in*—a cagelike sphere the size of a balled-up person,
and it gives him the look of a toy man someone
jammed inside a gyroscope. But, after all, he *is*
"the world"—he is, for Bruegel's purposes, the whole
deceitful globe. Yes, much the way the view of Antwerp
out the window of a prison in this other one, from 1562,
becomes the world—becomes a distant light-tinged scene,
so unattainable (the sails on the bay, the hovered gulls)
it comes to feel comprehensive of each single pleasure
life affords in every bend of land, in every friendly lump of bedding.
Melville's "Pequod" is intended as the world. And in the upstairs ward
the orderlies called No Return, I listened as a woman,

with enormous generosity, guided a tour through the stains
of her ceiling and walls, and through the abstract pattern
of her patched chenille bedspread—these, a detailed map
to the planet Eterna, and all of its seas, all of its basilica'd cities,
had their weighty, populated histories. "And this," she switched
attention to the lose-yourself-inside-it endless-viridian of a lamp's
ceramic glaze, "is outer space." She knew the birth and death
of every thumbprint galaxy. And the desk lamp
in Elizabeth Bishop's "12 O'Clock News" is wittily
transmogrified into a full moon; and the typewriter
into a terraced "escarpment" rising on "the central plain";
and a spilling pile of manuscripts, a landslide: as if *any*
of the Earth's minutiae might be DNA for replicating
Earth full-scale. This is why my marriage

disparages anything less than a Chinese New Year Dragon
(a beast of the gods as long as a city block, a whiskered river
with the bebop in its belly and a fire in its mad jaws) as a symbol;
and why we argue until the first pearl light of dawn hits
like a car crash on our skin, we're made that sensitive; and why
sometimes we're gentle the way the lid is to the eye. Because
we do it for you. Because we bear your grief and celebration
in our own, your dulling wits, your verve, your human juice.
Because our fury is Fury; and our woe is Woe; our love is Love.
John Hoyt was asked to remember thirty-five years back
to the set of that lo-budg quickie. "We had six or eight rocks
and some dead trees. We kept walking around and around them
while the prop men rearranged them," he said.
Eventually it was a continent.

Substratum

The Black Lagoon is turbid—is an inky egg-drop soup
of mysterious antediluvian matrix—and its famous Creature
doesn't rise up *from* it, but more accurately
is it, in the way a genie is one with the smoke in the lamp.
There's so much socio- and psychoacademic jaw-breeze
solely devoted to reasoning out the tropes of this
impressive ichthyterror, this ornately scaled and gilled
half-fish-half-man, that it's a challenge to reanimate
the goofy wonder of 1954 when I was six, and "wreaking havoc"
meant—I thought—the Creature stunk. But I remember,
with a clarity four decades hasn't darkened,
its balletic underwater scene with the beautiful
(and therefore, natch, imperiled) Julie Adams; as well as its slow,
forebodingly thunky lumber on land. And also
It Came from Beneath the Sea: a *giant* octopussish horror,
released from the aboriginal sea-ooze ("out of primordial depths"
the poster says) to smack the San Francisco skyline
into bloody rubble. And also *The Phantom from 10,000 Leagues*.
And also *The Beast from 20,000 Fathoms*. Lesson:
the substratum of things is seemingly everprolific
in monstrosity. It *squanders*
ogreish shapes, and can afford to. In *The She Creature,* Andrea,
standardly "gorgeous hypnotist's assistant," is regressed to her
most atavistic past-self: talons,
bony hooks, fangs, wings, antennae, fins, and a stomach cavity
framed in hokey tusklike teeth. *Forbidden Planet's* stunning nemesis
—a hungry, abstract "field" of "force" that kills—
is the scientist Morbius's unconscious mind
projected into the everyday light of exterior space:
an id
with the physical presence of Kong.
Well, that's the function of Hollywood (another way of saying
the function of myth): to *make* a thing

that large, to make it the size of a culture.
Once I drove with Ed up the Northwest coast, from sunrise
into stars: so there was time
for our initial series of wiseass, zinger badinage
to deepen. After one especially
empty silence, he said: "One night
when I was driving the old-time gin-joint back roads
in Kentucky—this would have been, geez, this would have been the spring
of 1983—I looked in my rearview mirror and saw a face
was floating in the darkness of the backseat. It was the face
of a demon. A virulent sulfur-green; and a malevolent grin.
I wasn't drunk or drugged or sleepy, the weather was clear.
And there was that face, as plain as a fist or an apple.
I'd turn around, and it was gone. I'd look in the mirror again,
and there it was again, as if some factory worker in Tokyo
had fixed it into the air of the car to begin with. Just silent.
Watching. Don't ask *me;* it came with me all the way
over the state line, and it stayed until the sun came up
outside of Cincinnati. That was the only time." We're quiet
for a while after that, my sane
and rational and civilized compadre Ed and me.
Our conversation shades away to the usual
rants, the usual guy enthusiasms, the usual instances
of highway philosophy over a styrofoam coffee cup,
the usual florid memories of women. Then we're quiet
again. Ed says: "When Helen and I divorced . . . shit,
when I found her fucking Gus in our bed that time,
it seared my mind for a long long while, I did some truly
malicious things in return. That spring when I lived in Kentucky,
I heard her mother died, and Helen needed me there
at the funeral. In fact I'd loved her mother too. And what
I did, out of spite?—I drove to see
an old ladyfriend in Ohio. A lot of ugliness
was trapped inside my brain, and needed *out.*"
It's then I share with him my hazy recollection of the story
of Paul and Annie Smith—and when I'm back home,
I look up the details. Three days after their marriage,
in April 1972, in Yorkshire, on their way to deliver
leftover wedding cake to a friend, their three-wheel mini-car
slammed straight-on into the rear of a truck, "went underneath,
came out and somersaulted several times, hitting a bus stop
and landing square on its nose." The couple survived, and in fact
had presence of mind enough to film the car immediately

for insurance purposes. Annie Smith: "When watching the film
for the first time, I saw someone in the passenger seat,
distinctly. It was terrifying." . . . *came to believe the image
was of a "crisis apparition" of Mrs. Smith, imprinted out of her,
onto the air, by her sharp, primal fear of death.*
And the eight grainy minutes of weirdly sinuous
something making lengths of sunset-gilded s's on the black scrolls
of Loch Ness. The giant golden turtle of Hoan Kiem Lake.
The dragon of Banyok, 250 miles northwest of Moscow,
ascending giddily from the depths of its liquid midden
for the timely tourist camcorders, snorting once
with Mesozoic hauteur, and then diving cleanly out of sight.
If *Creature from the Black Lagoon* is "a seminal,
even a monumentally seminal, cinematic text to study" . . . then
these jittery and blurred home-movie testaments are the graffiti
that our neighbors scrawl in their genuine way
around that monument's base. They always have,
from the beginning. When Leviathan arose from the waters.
When Snake Mother came from the [waves?] [sea?] (water sign).
And then does Tiamat rage (up) from the (place of) water,
from the First Abode, and the people are scattered,
their dwellings and their stores of grain are scattered,
they moan and Tiamat rages,
they beat at their breasts and Tiamat comes,
they beat at their heads and Tiamat rages.

Various Ulia

Did we say it out loud? Eventually
we said it. Cancer. Somewhere someone else
said AIDS. But only toward the last,
near the end, when the dying was
the fear—and not the dying's being invited.
For such is the power of utterance.
   Susie says that even ten years since the divorce,
she refuses to drive alone at night
—that's when the words come back.
   Although the infamous Mercury Theater production
of *The War of the Worlds* (October 30, 1938)
was intended to horrify, still,
"CBS cut the cries of the invading Martians
('Ulia, Ulia Ulia') as too frightening."
   A song comes on; she won't say why, but
she needs to turn off the radio.

Two Weeks, with Polo Chorus

Every culture has its own distinctive features; Chinese windmills turn hori-
zontally; in Istanbul, the scissors have hollow blades, and the luxury spoons are
made of wood from the pepper plant; Japanese and Chinese anvils are different
from ours; not one nail was used to build the boats on the Red Sea and the
Persian Gulf, and so on.
   —The Structures of Everyday Life, Fernand Braudel

She's upstairs assembling the lounga-recliner.
Strut C . . . into knob-slot A . . . then tighten . . .
From the dormer window, she can see him,
Mr. Mechanic, clucking over his bike—she can *observe* him
maternally tending its frailties, oiling it, and buffing it. . . .
Two weeks now, that they've known each other. Usually
it's a goofily pubescent thunkathunka loveorama feeling
filling her, but . . . just now, somehow,
watching as he lobs his toolbox
over the stone ledge into her bed of nasturtiums . . .
it's a fundamental *strangeness* she senses,
as his own needs and itineraries stake their alien claim
to the day . . . and suddenly this *uno*-a-*uno*
xenophobia won't let her go.

~

And Marco Polo says, in the city of Hormuz
ships are fastened not by iron nails but thread
from coconut husks, and caulked with fish oil
which we do not do here, and the Tartars, when they sit
to eat, they take their graven god and smear a lump of fat
around his mouth and the mouths of his wife and children
which we do not do here, and the idols of Cathay
and Japan and Manzi have the heads of cattle,
pigs, and dogs, and sheep, and some have three faces or four
and some a thousand hands *and these are not our gods,*
and in Cathay at the time of betrothal of marriage,
certain matrons especially deputized by both of the parties
will prove the bride's virginity (or not) by the test
of the pigeon egg *which we in our Christian land do not.*
—In Haiti in 1937, Royal Geographical Society member
Ian Sanderson wrote "I found here three bicycles
left by a stranded Circus that went broke,"
and the locals were using them to power their local
electrical dynamos: a savvy and almost familiar
otherusefulness which we do not do.

~

The story I want to tell you is one of hair in the sink,
of clock alarms that chitter someone else's
daily schedule through your sleep—of things
as minimal as the scribble of shit a guppy trails,
adding up unbearably. / She feeds his fish, and watches
the wavering drapery of flakes descend. . . . Alone upstairs,
he notices the lounga-recliner. Renee,
his ex, enjoyed a similar penchant
for unfolding the instructions (pidgin Martianese),
then flurrying into a wrench-and-lugnut tizzy. . . .
Renee, her ginger-speckled shoulders, and
her matching towel-and-loofah sets . . . That's history,
though. *This* lounga-recliner he's sitting in is
. . . and he drops through its ill-fit seat with a crash.

And Marco Polo says, in the city of Hormuz are professional
mourners, women who bewail the dead
on hire *which to us appears strange,* and
in the island Japan the dead are buried
with a pearl in the mouth, white or sometimes red
which is not our way, and among the Tartars
the practice is this, that when a boy will die
and in another family a girl will die of similar age,
a deed is arranged and the two are given
unto each other in matrimony *and this is not our custom,*
and in the city Sa-chau the dead are cremated,
and horses and camels of paper, and pieces of money of paper
are burnt so that the dead may have these
truly with them in the next life *even though*
this is peculiar to us, and in the city Khan-balik
the money is made of the bark of mulberry trees,
and in Kaindu province the money is loaves of salt,
and in the province of Toloman the money is cowrie shells,
and more, and further, and ever else, *and this is not*
our way our righteous way our sweet familiar.

~

Words—not a quarrel exactly, but . . . words
with edges. He slammed the door (a kind of overword)
and now he's out riding. She's here, she's watching
three beautiful fecal ideograms three guppies drag,
some untranslatable statement through the water.
He's out riding . . . he's out burning it away
on the bike. *Away* is the point: the piling up of distance.
But a psychic thread connects him
to her house and can't be shaken off; the farther he goes,
the fiercer he pedals, the stronger is its wirey pull
and the more his energy seems to light the house
he leaves behind. Two weeks, and already they make
a system. He remembers eighth-grade science: how
the term they use to measure electric current is *resistance.*

True

Of Devotion / John Donne

There is, in ev'ry Temple to Our Lord,
A Portion of His worshippers who raise
Their voices, where from Deep Within is pour'd
Into the world Great, Tributarie Prayse;
The whiles their Thought is contemplating Else,
Of Merchantry, or Spite, or Carnal ways;
And thus, their song of Reverence is false,

—speaking of which, I'd better stop here and admit
(not that I necessarily think it was a world-class con)
I wrote those lines. No one likes being lied to
—though with history behind us, and with politics to left and right,
we're used to it by now. We know that Plato would bar poets
from the gates of his ideal state, essentially because they "lie"
(see pseudo-Donne above, as current evidence); about the time
that Vasco da Gama reached India, the Chinese
made construction of an oceangoing junk a crime, and burned
the logbooks of earlier ships, because explorers trafficked in
"deceitful exaggerations of bizarre things." Don't we all,
as the night grows thick around our tongues, and the face
of the clock on the wall of the bar refuses to flinch, no matter
what full crock it overhears. What Plato fears

is accurate enough: unchecked, our natural attraction
toward embellishing (or outright whopperstyle re-creating)
what a friend here calls "the actualfactual true poop"
will confound our lives past any sane decision-making.
"THIS," a woman screamed out, fueled by enmity and whiskey sours,
"this," and "this" again, as if the noun to come were too foul
to approach without a sputtered string of buffering, "this
'marriage' is a *fiction,* is a goddamn Halloween-mask SHAM!"
Though the party guests ducking her room-trajecting highball glass . . .
was real. If this smacks of glammy TV shockumentaries,
it's had its quiet counterpart in every heart I know: a lonely
moment when the I.D. card of Who We Are Inside at last
won't match the face we daily show the world. Then
endless floatingdrowningfalling in our myriad ways. And yet

the truly nutso charm of fakery can't be denied:
the faddish rich in the middle of the nineteenth century
had their landscaped grotto installations decorated with old men
dressed as "Gothic" hermits moping around in retro-fashion cassock and cowl.
And some of this less-than-verity is *hilarious,* by which I mean
for example the phone-sex caller who complained that when he dialed
the "Hear Me Moan" line, what he got was a recording of a woman
nagging her husband. (The telephone standards committee then ruled
that the tape met its title's criteria.) Some lies not only nubble
extra texture in our lives, they *save* our lives: I know
a couple in their eighties now who snuck from Hitler's Germany
as corpses, in a rattling van of many hundreds of *real* corpses
being hauled for fertilizer: "We rode into life in the arms
of the dead," he says. "In the *smell* of the dead," she adds,

and then: "For years I dreamed that I *was* dead. I would wake up
screaming and not understand—for how could a *cadaver* scream?"
Extreme—but representative of that faceted thing
we call the human psyche. We'd better get used to it,
aren't we all collagework, every "me" complete
with zip-out not-me lining, every "solid" "thing" a fizz
of void and quantum physics hocuspocus, isn't the green we see as "leaf"
the light the leaf refuses, not the light it *is?*
You needn't be the Prince of Bigamists or a Secret Service plant
in an enemy embassy to understand instinctively
that "you" is forever a lie to every equally credible
"alter-you" . . . and *then*
what's verifiable, what senses do we trust? A story
from out of the life of Donne, as reported by Izaak Walton:

round with child, afeared, Anne Donne allows his travel to France
on an ambassadorial mission with a faint
"unwilling willingness." The second night in Paris, Donne looks up
from the table and sees "my.dear wife pass twice by me,"
hair in wild disarray "and a dead child in her arms."
A servant is sent back to London and twelve days later returns
with the news that "Mrs. Donne [is] very sad and sick
. . . she had been delivered of a dead child." Yes, and *did*
Donne "see" "her"? Water into water, and who can tell
the demarcations? Snow in more snow, and in yet more snow,
and dark poured like an unguent into dark, and time
on top of time, and "truth" spilled into "history."
I picture him in a study that night, remembering an incomplete
erotic sonnet he started for her, so many life-upheavals ago. . . .

> We hie to bed, the way that they go Forth
> Who seeke New Lands, who test the falsitie
> Of Rivers running Gold, and test the Worth
> Of tales of Beasts that Speake. And if they then Bee
> Lost inside this New and Rich Countrie,
> They have their Lodestone. We have ours and we
> Do not fear therefore. Love is our True north. . . .

Directional

↓

The level where the bits of frizzled-out satellites orbit
isn't "high up"—not in a universe that reaches unboundedly out
to the flimmering skins of forming and dying
stars, the ghosts of stars, the great creation-wisps of stars . . .
it makes the swifts, this April evening, as they dive
and lift in zippy bug-gulp passes that we think
should trail scorchmarks through the air . . . it makes
these remarkable flyers ("overhead," "in the sky")
mere bottomgrubbers, not markedly different from us,
from everyone bearing the umpty-ump impossible tons of atmosphere
per square inch on their bodies. And the rain
"falls" "down." The leaves, in their season. The snows.
The light on this page has been falling for 93 million miles.
Think of everything it carries by the time it lands.
In Kansas, in the flatlands here, a farmhouse sits in the middle
of such emptiness, such morning-misted and borderless space,
below such *outer* space, that from the distance of the interstate
it looks like a corner of sunken Atlantis,
tilted a little, weaved through by the sea-floor things
that have no eyes and live on flakes of sediment. And even

≈

↑

here, the idea of "up" is alive, and people wake—or, as they say,
they "rise"—routinely from a dream of flying. Some
of them levitate casually, as if they sat on top
of an invisible pillar elevating. Others run and flap their arms
like one of da Vinci's apprentices strapped to a hinged contrivance.
One friend says: "I met him in midair, we fucked
in zero-gees like . . . dandelion-fluff with a sex drive!" These
are the secular versions of what we see in the varnish-browns
of a sixteenth-century Flemish oil: people's bodies
sprawl the ground like shrimp husks, broken open
with a single cracking twist; and from this shell
a hazy spiral floats, that starts itself to take the shape
of a body; only, a spiritual body. See?—its eyes
look inward, it ascends with boneless pliancy.
The painter seems to say that what are wings
on other creatures are internalized for us
as sweet and aching alleluias in our breasts, and there
will come a Trump, a Judgment, and a Night of Din and Lightning
by which these will be released. And so the gravity
that claims us, and a counterbeckon heavenward, achieve

~

←⟶

a tensile balance: we're complex enough for these to coexist
in us. The late tenth-century Magyar ruler Géza
"continued to sacrifice to his ancient idols while,
at the same time, praying to Christ and sincerely taking the sacraments,
saying that he was rich enough to serve
two different gods." —As are we all, if *rich* is daily measured
by connection-dots that blip inside our brains, or by
the quicksand in our hearts. And though it's true that monotheism
makes a lesser thing, a "devil," an "evil prince," from what was once
in the older religions a god—an equal-powered god—that new demotion is only
taxonomy: our *real* lives, as we feel them in the small raw
human yolk at our psychic centers, always offer themselves to more
than one force at a time. This snappy, street-sly
six-year-old, as one example: scampering the alley
with a kite and roll of string; *and* with a gram of asskick coke
crimped into her sneaker. Her daddy's at home, "getting high."
Her momma's on the shrink's couch, "feeling low." This
diametric pull-apart we see graphed-out in her
so vividly is only a single instance of (truly) everybody's apposite
and simultaneous weathers. When the main electrical plant

∽

for the entire city died, *kaput,* and some blocks went ten days
until that juice returned, and people lived
a huddled-at-the-fireplace existence that was barely
twentieth century, "have you got power?" soon replaced
"how are you?" as a greeting until it took on the loose and mystical
aura of having a capital *P;* and in the unlit night,
they'd catch themselves unconsciously looking away from the city generator
across the bay, and up to the fires-spotted expanse of the sky,
as if *this* might be the source of their answer.
So it goes. We bury our parents, deep—and think that they continue
to instruct us from "on high." We bear the weight of one more year
each year, we shlep our day's frustrations on our back
—then fall in love and "walk on air." The crazy evidence
is everywhere. At the bend in the alley I came across an old
abandoned floor safe, of the kind that might have once stored
the entire office assets of an 1890s robber baron: sizable and heavy
enough to hold the deed on every swatch of deforested land in the continent.
Someone had tied it up with kite twine; maybe that girl I saw.
It won't fly. It won't ride the wind. Yet, somehow . . . even
here, even this, smacks faintly of resurrection.

generations

"Duo Tried Killing Man with Bacon"
—headline, *The Spokesman Review* (Spokane, WA)

At tornado force, a full length of uncooked spaghetti
has skewered a heart, and killed. A falling block
of frozen urine. A trout, that leaped precisely
into a yawn and thrashily lodged until the breath stopped.
Endless ways. Perhaps each death is as unique as the life
it ends, to whatever extent that is. I do know
when they found the fourteen corpses in the rubble
of the pipe-bombed synagogue, that mass of broken and indistinguishable flesh
was still divided equally into enough for fourteen burials,
and each of the families' griefs was its own. My father didn't need this

immediate neighborhood drama: fear of what the world could do
to his family was a living writhe inside him; once I doodled it
as a liver fluke that could mimic the face,
as needed, of my sister, mother, self. Because Chicago
offered its perils in generous headline-shrilling quantity
(and some—like the parts of children they always seemed to be finding
dumped in shallow graves—were fiercely lurid) and because
the cells of the body so often and fatally
rebel against the whole . . . he lived his days out in a series
of preventive ceremonial gestures, alternately sacred or tepidly humdrum,

as a situation called for—or, as a character in the gypsy slums
of nineteenth-century London says, by way of exemplification, "I made warding signs
and said 'Garlic!' about a dozen times" (Tim Powers, *The Anubis Gates*).
Garlic guards against the evil eye, as does (depending on where you live)
a desiccated frog, a shamrock, bezoar stones removed from the stomach of llamas,
handsigns like the "horns" or the "fig," or ritual spitting.
Beeswax candles. Lamb's blood over the door. My father
set my weekend curfew, and heeded the vast refusals of kosher laws,
etc., sternly certain that these self-set limits saved us from the limitless
predations of the universe. I think of what Tim Meiseneltzer felt

—the "victim"—manacled, ankles and wrists, on the floor of the woods,
and a bagful of fat-edged rashers spread around his body
to attract the local wolves. He lived. And it was even comic
in its way. But what did he feel, *then,* with the kicking
hoof of death in his chest. With the fist of death in his rectum
slowly opening up. Its taloned glove. What promise did he breathe
to what protector-god. I *can't* think into that
alien fear. But I remember a version of its minor key: my father
accidentally biting into a BLT, then kneejerk spitting it out
in a cafeteria napkin, while the whole world watched, and the heavens

stared down, as if our lives depended on this.

The Fiction Shelf

The Swiss watch isn't ticking for a week, before
a credible Hong Kong knockoff's on the market.
Fraud has always been a close, close shadow.
A blink or two after there's money, there's
counterfeit money: the fake of a silver coin
from the island of Aegina is sixth-century B.C.
In medieval Egypt, an inspector called
"the censor of morals" oversaw quickie eatery stalls, where
mystery extender in the rolled meats wasn't rare.
Presumably Eve would sometimes mimic the crescendo
of pleasure, and Adam his longing—anyway
certainly *after* the Expulsion. It's always pacing us,
it's always almost *ahead* of us: some shrewdly suited,
loitering imposter awaiting an impostee.

~

This ochered spoke of bone . . . This bony hole
it *nearly* fits, but doesn't fit . . . *Is*
Piltdown Man the greatest hoax of the twentieth century?
—all of those high minds brought to low blows
in persnickety scholarly tiffing. No,
a friend insists, the absolute whopper of all would be
that great granddaddy of "pyramid schemes"
the dapper swindler Ponzi perpetrated in 1920. . . .
Whatever. We pay the check, go home
to our respective simulations of daily contentment.
I have friends I love whose marriages are compounded
of cosmetics, aluminum siding, and scripted avowal . . .
then the curtain drops, their audience leaves, and in an itchy aversion
they unfasten their intricate happiness masks.

~

In 1897, when Peary returned to New York from another
triumphant Polar expedition, he brought six visiting
Greenland Eskimos, too—a sort of informal and very "proto"
cultural exchange trip. Four of the Eskimos died,
but a child, Mene, and Uisakavskak, an adult,
returned to their people in the spring of 1898.
Uisakavskak regaled the tribe with his tales
of "houses as big as icebergs; people
live up in the air like auks on a cliff.
There are so many of them, when people make breakfast
the smoke rises out of their chimneys until the sun
is eclipsed." And the elder angrily shouted at him,
"Uisakavskak, go tell your big lies to the women!"
He had lost their respect, and was given the name "Big Liar."

~

Do we need *more* newsreel footage?—bodies
tossed in carts like sheaves of shitted rags,
and the bereaved in the dirt. They've been led here,
of course, by one of the various Great Untruths
the sachems of our world dispense like penny candy.
Other untruths are smaller but kinder, and one
of the newsreels features lines of weary, war-torn
refugees passing a gaudy gypsy wagon,
where a healing tomorrow is hokily predicted
for a pear or crust. I know a man who lives in lavish
Xanadus of lies lies lies, self-mesmerized,
believing them, they're such a heartstabbingly beautiful
contradistinction. We've been hurt enough;
the right lie is redemptive.

~

18 people in a room. "I love you" each says to another, meaning
18 different things . . . 1,800 different things . . . 7 *continents*
of different things. . . . A public word is already only
a fiction of its referent. This spatting couple, up
all night in talk made from divisiveness . . .
What do I wish for them—some monolithic verity
to share? You know there isn't one. You know
that it's a world of slippery relativism we fumble through,
a universe of subatomic "here" and "not-here" blips.
But I can wish, at least, they share a lie—a single
and emollient lie, like a bottle of herbal Cure-All Wonder Waters
from the gypsy wagon; thus do we calm and anchor
our lives, that the periodic table of elements
ceaselessly reinvents.

≈

"*Poo-jok,*" their Eskimo guide said—"mist."
But MacMillan and Green were sure they witnessed
"hills, valleys, snow-capped peaks," at last
the fabled Arctic Atlantis, "Crocker Land," that Peary
recorded having seen just a few degrees from the Pole
in 1906. It was eight years later now, and they headed
relentlessly toward it—over shifting, grinding
crash-ice, and into a wind that sometimes halted
the forward-straining dogs like a wall. Their party
required four more years to return. They were 14,000 1917-dollars
over budget. Green had shot Pee-a-wah-to,
the Eskimo guide, to death in an ice-blind madness.
And of course there was no Crocker Land.
Deluded by *poo-jok*—broken by mist.

≈

So many moments leave us feeling emptied-out
and helpless, while the con-game packs its shill-stuffs
into the idling van. . . . My mother lightly places
her hand on my arm: *Opnarn iz keyn kunts nit,*
she says: "Deceiving others is no big trick."
I find this homily consoling somehow—its Yiddishy
sense of community, her attempt at comforting
contact. Then: *Der bester lign iz der emes,*
she says: "The best lie is the truth." I don't really
understand that; still, it has the ring of something
solid and true. I'm glad she's visited. But
my mother is dead. I've mumbled over her gravestone.
Now her touch disappears from my arm
—she's spirited back to the land of isn't.

!!!The Battle of the Century!!!

the handbills shrill, in searing orange-crimsons. *Any* century.
There will always be these two opponents, circling for a throat-hold.
Call them Plus; and Minus. Call them Void; and Matter
(from before there even *were* "centuries," or any creatures
capable of notching an antler into a lunar calendar).
Sperm; and Ovary. Belief; and Doubt. Thrift; and Bounty.
Steady-state; and Ever-expanding. Curse; and Blessing. *Versus*
is the only engine possible under the physical laws of our universe.
Slyly hip to this most elementary of verities,
the carny barkers are briskly pitching the wonders
of that asterisk-heralded titular battle scheduled for noon
in the center tent, twixt Dragon Sam, the Great Exhaler
of Gouts of Amazing Flame (whose claim
was, he could "conflagrate to the length
of four bull elephants trunk-to-tail," and for a coda
"thrust a white-hot coal inside his fundament, as a suppository"); and
Liquid Dan, the Living Geyser, Fountain of Fantastic Feats
(and who, in fact, could down a hundred mugs, then spout
a grandly arching shower into a silver basin twenty feet away,
"and you will see this stream change into a series of rainbow colors").
Fire; and Water. The ancient story. And so
the tent can barely hold the crowd.
And isn't this—because it's 1800—just a sideshow version
of the clash between the Neptunists and the Vulcanists
at scholarly colloquia? Such contumely
heaped like buckets of rhinoceros dung by stammering men of letters
over one another's anger-reddened heads!
". . . will clearly demonstrate, for all time, and beyond *all skepticism*"
[here, a glare of poison spear-tips at his colleague with the whiskers]
"that the agents of geological change have been—since the Creation,
to the Present Day—the rising and recession of the Waters,
and the work of Rain and of Rivers upon the land.
As to the specious, vapid, dunce-expounded theory

of the primacy of" [forcing out a jackass laugh] "volcanic action
evidenced at all . . ." [*Rah! Rah!* and *Bah! go soak
your beanbrain in your Waters!* and *Tell them, Chauncey!*]
at which, the bewhiskered proponent of Lava and Magma leaps up
to the podium, as heated as his subject, and: "You demonstrate
the intellect of a tuber!" [*Huzzah!* and also some *Boo!* and a single
Let them go at each other with rowboat oars!] "The work,
the immemorial work, of the Fires . . ." "Charlatan!" "Pestilential lout!"
[*and then it all breaks down beneath the weight of assorted professorial
catcalls, thrown tomatoes, hoots, and mooshed-in noses*]—
Scene: A Farmer; and a Cattleman.
Monotheism; and Pantheon. Electric; and Acoustic. There will always be
the bringing forth of Light, from Dark, and then a cosmos built
on that division. There will always be two sixteen-year-old lovers
screwing madly, for the contrast, on top of a grave.
Scene: He's back at the house, from the pasture. There's
this moment in his day—the sheep are tallied-up, and penned;
the silo, locked; the children, safely, even quietly,
at their various indoors busyness—when everything seems to fit
foursquare in its own ordained container, and the sky is the color
a rose is, and the dusk against his face is like another face,
familiar, soft. And then—what does it? a kind of sound?
some reminiscent whiff?—he has an image of the cattle ranchers
surging over everything, and suddenly aversion is a sickness
in his belly, is *a taste,* and hatred roils through his forehead
from a place in him so deeply lodged in Time, there aren't solids yet,
or sentience, and protein wars with protein.

∼

There's nothing. Then there's something. In terms of narrative
this is a rudimentary plot, this is The First Plot. Then
uncountabillion years go by: the story is the same now,
but the players are gods and primal monsters:
"Nothing existed, there was nothing," says the *Popul Vuh,*
"and in this nothing the Creators waited, the Maker,
Tepeu, Gucumatz. They planned the whole creation of everything,
arguing . . ." Yes: *arguing.* For energy requires
a polarity, define it how you will. When two millennia go by
it's 1939, and *Marvel Mystery Comics* #1 is on the stands
and introduces its credulous adolescent audience to The Human Torch
(whose body is that, essentially, of a Superman flambé;
who hurls his fireballs—like snowballs, see? only fire—
with force enough to burn through steel, and can ensnare
the nefarious crimelords of his day in webs of fire,
or trap them in barrels of fire, etc.; who's solemnly sworn
to use his combustible powers "for justice!"; who can fly, because
"the combined blue and red flames made The Human Torch
lighter than air," a surely physics-revisioning concept) AND . . .
to The Sub-Mariner [as in *marinate,* not *marine*]
(who is really Prince Namor of Atlantis, undulant son
of the subsea royalty, ocean-breather, and commander
of the waves to do his bidding—and by extension, waters
everywhere—as well as his endless subservient conscriptees
of true fish, shellfish, and the occasional ocean-dwelling mammal, and
who can fly because of tiny wings on either heel).
Each premiered in a separate sock-and-pow adventure, of which he was the star,
but unlike calls to unlike, over barriers
of distance and time, with the undeniable inner pull
of gravity or magnetism: Matter; and Antimatter.
Cops; and Robbers. Done; and Meant-to-do. By July of 1940
the two are sparring with a grim, persistent hydro/pyro-inevitability
that so far—with lapses and revivals—has lasted over fifty years.
The ill-tempered Namor could *never* be lazily plotting any aqueous mischief
in his "self-appointed castle, the Statue of Liberty," *without*
The Human Torch, on serendipitous patrol above, besieging him
with fireballs, their snakily prehensile tails of cartoon-red
across the cartoon-blue of the New York skies. "I'll douse you yet,
you raging hothead!"—with a shaking fist. They made a holistic system.
Point; and Counterpoint. This hectoring, from a single issue:
"You flaming fool!" "You water rat!" "This is the end of you,
my little glo-worm!" "Here! I've got you at last, my fine
water-moccasin!" "Fire-bug!" "Water-bug!"—shibboleths

by which they know each other in a world they both find alien
(after all, they're both a super-brand of freak) or almost,
almost like the babytalk of lovers, or the weird, parodic
babytalk of lovers when their lust and loathing grip the same
whipped nerves: "Come on, you big fish!"
"I'm coming, Flame!"—and they're indistinguishable.
Continuing that interrupted sentence from the *Popol Vuh:*
"They planned the whole creation of everything, arguing
each point until their words and thoughts crystallized and became
the same thing." Though I earlier fashioned a comic scene
of rivalrous exchange between the Neptunists and Vulcanists,
the partisans of each were sober men engaged in sober labor
over years of thought, and of scrupulous fieldwork—the nascent labor
by which our comprehensive twentieth-century understanding
of geologic change was formed. To imagine these seasoned scholars, volleying
their invective—! "It is indefensible. . . ."
"Even a child would laugh at such impoverished reasoning. . . ."
Finally, posterity wedded them.

∾

For forty years, my mother lay down at my father's side each night.
Now ten years after his death, we lay her there again.
If "her" is a viable construct, under the circumstances
—or "there." And what about "self"? And "who"? For instance,
to "who" did my sister talk, those several gray and rainy minutes
after the shovelwork was done and the dirt was level?
You can say a dozen different things, and none of them will change
the biochemical fact, the noise we are, the silence we become.
No matter *what* the question is, the real answer
is death. So: 2 + 2 = death. The major export of Fill-in-the-Blank,
and who did I see you with last night, and the number of feet in a mile:
death death death. It's surely the answer to where
we go in sex, the way our concentration
on the body—all of its anthers lit like Vegas,
all of its cellar kitchens spooning up a funky musk-alfredo—
pulses suddenly, and empties us out of our "us,"
out of our "here," and into some free-floating "where"
so atemporal, we could be motes in the sun
of Sumeria, or the dander of the twenty-fifth century
thermaling over the rocketports . . . wherever, it's the unguessable place
—if "place" is a viable construct—that my mother went
as the nurse held her wrist and the tiny molecular fuelpile
finished its countdown. This is vague,
I know, but no worse so than the rational alternative
that traditional Science offers us: the swarming
entomology necropolis, then a redistribution
back to the world as combinable protoparticles. Okay,
swell. Or Religion: those delicate human-headed *ba*-birds
hovering over the chests of the recently entombed
in ancient Egyptian art are charming images, equally so
are the willowy ectoplasmic shapes escaping like bouquet
from uncorked wine, in medieval and Renaissance scenes, but . . . none of it's
going to comfort my niece as she walks from her grandmother's funeral service
dutifully to the waiting limo. None of it means
a thing to the skin she lives in. On the homemade bier they carpentered
for Dragon Sam, a circus poster artist painted perfect scroll-like flames
around the panels, as a tribute to his famous, florid talent,
but this, as always, is eloquent more of our need for ritual
than it is of our understanding of what's "beyond";
the mourner's Kaddish we said in that afternoon rain, we said
for ourselves. And when it was over?—I lingered
as the limo's windows misted and its engine purred pure silk.
I listened, hard. Two voices fought for attention. "The Emperor

Q'in Shih-hunang-ti was buried with life-size terracotta figures
of an army of over 1,400 warriors (including a section of cavalry
with chariots). It's amazing here, in me, where your mother is
now. There is no death here; only the dead, which is different.
Only the bones: the stopped batons. Only the music
written for scarab-shears and petroleum forming. I'm the one weight,
and she's a part of that weight. Look down—" and the other voice
broke in, "Look up." I did: the sun was like a gold yolk
being folded into gray dough. There were morphing shapes,
as usual, whatever I wanted: continents, fantastic beasts,
continual reorganization—"Everyone was here at the first,
and is here at the last," this voice said, "and then here at the first
again: do you understand?" "No, no; look down, and breathe
the nearly carnal richness from between a mushroom's pleats. . . ." And so
they vied this way, they wanted me, as if the shitty penny
of belief that I could offer were the universe's treasure.
—Each, beseeching allegiance.
Earth; and Air.

Con Carne

*We might also follow fashion in food through the revealing history of . . . "good"
and "bad" ways of roasting meat—but that is another, and very long, story.*
—*The Structures of Everyday Life,* Fernand Braudel

My father had worked ten-hour days from when he'd turned sixteen,
he lugged the blending tubs, then finally sold accounts,
my mother had disciplined herself to the needs
—the nearly pre-electric needs—of a 1940s kitchen
for that long as well, but this was new, in fact
this was The First Time, on The First Day of their real life
together, that he drove the bumping 1947 Chevy home
to a wife along an imagined thread of the odor
of pot roast she had done, for him, as he
had shmoozed the sorry shit of the world for her, for only her,
with the lovingcare of a meisterjeweler
sculpting a diamond under his loupe. / That hunger
was here at the start. We've found the shankbones
charred in the hearths of *Homo erectus,* "Peking man,"
400,000 years ago, and it must have been common
protoculinary practice even then. The bones
—they're human bones—were roasted, and then cracked
to reveal the yellow oily glisten of their marrow inside:
the last, perhaps the richest, of the body's held-back secrets
to be fingered out into the emberlight, as if
this early lesson is that the music *is in* the baton,
the magic *is in* the wand,
and embodiable. / For some, the sudden
cochineal jungle at the center
of a medium-rare filet mignon. For some,
their strip of Reser's Bull Whip Pepper Stix, *a yard*
of jerkied whatsit beef. In the year 1000,
"people ate cranes, storks, swans, crows, herons, and loons,"
and the monks of the abbey of St. Gall "treated their guests
to the barbeque of a complete horse." When the Traveler
reravels his way back home to the England of H. G. Wells
from the year 802,701 A.D., "For a time
my brain went stagnant. Presently I got up

and came through the passage here, I saw the *Pall Mall Gazette*
on the table, I found the date was indeed today,
and looking at the timepiece, saw the hour was almost eight o'clock.
I heard your voices and the clatter of plates. I hesitated
—I felt so sick and weak. Then I sniffed
good wholesome meat, and opened the door on you."
/ The browning we see in roasting occurs
when certain amino acids and sugars are subject to dry heat
—this is called "the Maillard effect," and this
is what's responsible for the typical enticing aroma
that gets the mouth wet like a lover. / "My ass
is what got me hired," my cousin Deedee once said of her summer job
as a carhop at Teddybear Burger—the shirred skirt always eager
to billow a peekaboo froth around her hips—
"and got me *boocoo* tips" if she would only titter at the obvious
sophomore wit surrounding "buns," and she did, she was always the frisky,
risky, high-hormonal, lust-struck baby of the family,
I never saw her waste good indignation
on a problem that her estrogen
could handle much more keenly, "but all that ended," and this
is the closest I ever heard her approach a principled feminist ire,
"when I wouldn't suck off the night manager, and
they put me on day shift standing out in the street in 98°
in the Burger Bear costume." / Tartar warriors
stashing a slab of the day's kill under the saddles
of their sturdy steppes-bred ponies, and then after another
long-ridden day of marauding . . . *voilà!*—automatic supper
of coarse-ground game, served raw (from which,
our "steak tartare"), discreetly seasoned
"with oil of saddle and sweat of horse's rump." What
won't we relish. "The liver of a walrus
is a delicious morsel. Fire would ruin
the curt and pithy vitality which belongs to its uncooked pieces."
"The flesh of the rat is here considered an able
hair-restorer." Starving in the Gobi,
Lord Dunn-Nulworthy boiled a camel's hoof
"for three days, until it was serviceable." / He
could picture the sanctum awaiting him; at least
that's how their two-flights-up apartment near the el tracks asked
to image itself at the end of a day of snafus stacked
past bearing—belts of sprockets torn,
the time sheets stolen . . . *cheez louise,* a chunk of granite
would drop its stoic demeanor and kvetch at *tsooris* like this.

And after all, my father was only human. He was at the corner
of State & Division, idling in back of a semi and thinking wistfully
of the checkerboard linoleum in their kitchen, and a beckoning
weather of roast-scent in the air there, and a woman who would take him
somewhere inside of herself a thousand miles away
from daily tumult . . . when the Chevy, with a sludge-glupped
mind of its own, bucked forward into the truck, unhousing
over fifteen crates of very startled chickens into the blattering
crawl of rush hour . . . and, by the time he finally,
wearily, entered their living room, he didn't need to hear
that her First Supper of Their Marriage had come to resemble
a pile of hockey pucks and carrot-colored marbles. Nor
did she need his mood. No, neither of them
really needed the looks of the other. / Marco Polo
reports that the Tartars boil their meat
in an animal's stomach, "and then they eat it 'pot and all.'"
On the other hand, he reports that "those who are called by this name
of *Yogi* would not kill any living creature,
neither fly nor flea nor louse. They do not eat anything
fresh, not herb or root, until it is dried, and only then;
because while they are green they have souls." / Exquisite,
these: The softening petals of boiled brisket
wafting off the soupbone. Near-black, leathery
shingles of pemmican. Nuggets of flank steak
carmelizing inside a glaze of onion baste.
A mound of chile-powdered *carne* as vibrant as henna.
The Olduvai layers of sausage-and-eggplant lasagna.
Goulash. Schnitzel. Hobo hash.
The obelisk of gyros. / It was a woman,
Elizabeth Rosin supposes: "Evidence seems to indicate
that the primitive olfactory brain is more highly developed
in females." So it happens: as the band of hominids
straggles across the savanna, their she-leader's sense
of smell is snagged by something new this afternoon,
it masses, pops, and thickly shimmers off the carcass of a young gazelle
that snapped a leg and roasts now in a dying heat
left over in these lightning-blasted grasses.
And the drip of its sweet succulence is smeared across
the grins of human faces
for the first time. Now whenever they can repeat this
happy recipe of fire and prey, they will. With an eel.
A squatty kind of hare. A calf. An eland.
With the prisoner they take from a similar band

of hominids and kill with stones. / He'd shoot them
with a gun if he could, but there aren't guns yet
(there are barely—by the standards of time a rock keeps,
or the breathable air—opposable thumbs yet). Terrified
and snuffling, he peeks out over the cover a brushy mound provides.
They've killed his cave-kin, Ta of the Quick Tongue, and he watches
as they gather to divide the corpse, while one
stands guard for even larger predators than they are. Rah
is weak now from the recent battle—he'd barely escaped—
and, tentatively safe in the brush, he slips off into a spasmy sleep. . . .
Then wakes. They're gone; some boar or lion has scattered the group.
Rah sniffs: an odor is in the air, a fragrance . . . something
greasily luxurious and undeniable lures him
to snatch at those lukewarm remains, to lift them (gingerly
at first, and then with educated frenzy)
to his lips . . . and does he know, does he suspect . . .
in any case, he can't refuse this thing that calls to him
as flesh calls flesh, what Charles Lamb
a gazillion years in the future will term "a kind
of animal manna. . . . [F]at and lean . . . that both together
make but one ambrosian result." / And what *does*
the Traveler find in 802,701 A.D. that makes his homecoming scene
so sharp in contrast?—"The place, by the by,
was very stuffy and oppressive, and the faint halitus
of freshly shed blood was in the air. Some way
down the central vista was a little table of white metal,
laid with what seemed a meal. Even at the time, I remember
wondering what large animal could have survived
to furnish the red joint I saw. I had a vague sense
of something familiar. . . ." / Stir-fried.
Curried. Teriyakied. Coiled in tortellini: a garden snail
of ground round. Also the *Kobe* beef of Japan:
beer-fed and hand-massaged, until the flavor is beyond
the tongue's ability to comprehend. And who can forget
that pair of five-feet trumpeter swans at the Levinsons' wedding,
sculpted out of chopped liver. / *"Would you like fries
with that?* I said it a stinking thousand times a day,
to every asshole with eighty-five cents. So when he answered
No, I'd like the cash in the register, and waved a gun, I knew
I was in love. I grabbed the money, I ran to his car with him,
and for two weeks after there wasn't a burger shack in Louisiana or Oklahoma
that was safe from us." / Norman was divorced in '67,
and in these thirty years he's never remarried; the other three

are widowers, Sol, Leroy, Yablowsky. Every morning at 7 A.M. they meet
at the Golden Arches, where they kvetch and kibbitz and generally opine
and put the shine on the jive, for at least two hours. *Every*
morning. Snow up to the nutskies doesn't stop them,
neither did the midtown flood in the spring of '80. "It's more
my home than my *home* is," Sol once said, and Norman
added "Yeah, and fewer of them cockroaches." If you think perhaps
the universe is founded on the basic elements oxygen and hydrogen,
or on a crystalline lattice, or is sturdily borne on the backs
of a series of turtles-on-turtles, I give you instead
its true, eternal square of infrastructure:
four coffees and breakfast patties. / Dickens
says of a novice butcher: "His very hair
seemed to have suet in it, and his fresh complexion
to be lubricated by large quantities of animal food."
One hundred years later, that boy, and his sister, are still parading
—as flecked as ever—around the Yards in Chicago.
"Me, I'm in Sliced Bacon. That's what some girls get,
it's lighter and cleaner. But some girls get Dry Casings,
where the pickle water eats away their nails, and eats
salt ulcers in their skin. One girl I knew was in Wet Casings,
where they string the pig guts over a pipe and run cold water through them,
she stood in that water past her ankles all day,
and the stink was still like a pomade stuck in her pores on Saturday night.
The men work Hog Kill, Beef Kill, Sheep Kill,
one man cuts off the head all day, another pulls fat off the carcass
and packs it into vats. A job like that,
it gets between your teeth, it gets in your eyes like sleep,
it makes your own children gag. And then at a Company picnic
we'd be scrubbed for once, with a pat of perfume . . .
the foreman grabs at our asses, like we
was cutlets being inspected." / Okay, so Norman
divorced her. Or she divorced *him.* By now the bridge of tears
and disappointment is so *looong,* she can't look back and see it
clearly. Okay, so now what? Now she's bought a little
carhop burger drive-in, and her friends are up past midnight with her
trying to rename it. "Belly Burger." "Biggie Burger."
"Buster Burger." "Hey, how about Bathos Burger?" "How about
next time you buy a brain, you thump it to see if it's ripe?"
"Brain Burger." "Teddybear—nah." Wait . . . yes,
yes, *Teddybear Burger,* and someone dressed like "Burger Bear"
enticing traffic into her lot! / Haiku:
A bar of Brahms.

A line from Dante.
A skewer of perfect kebab. /
I have nothing against the tofu burger. It doesn't,
however, sing to us in our dreams, and say those things
that fill the mouth with drool and pull at the blood
the way the full moon draws the cresting waters, it isn't
a synonym for our own dear flesh. / *Creamed calves' brain*
—from the recipe book of Apicius, circa 30 A.D. /
In Cairo, in 1400 A.D., "they cook a whole sheep,
and after it is done, a man will carry it
on his shoulders, with a table on his head,
and he goes through the streets in search of patrons, crying
'Who wants to eat?' " / Its aroma is a pleasure
to the nostrils of the Lord. Its aroma could ascend
on pillars of smoke as thick as the pillars of the Parthenon,
and still the Lord—not unlike His created ones—
would ask (or roar as if the very heavens spoke as a lion)
for more. "The fatted calf the people brought to the stone,
and it was an offering." This beef upon the altar is what
the gods elect to smell from us
instead of a rose or a bundle of fennel—*this,*
"the choice of the flocks," is what they grab up,
what they bend to. As do we, of course,
in their image. / "Well, the mood didn't last." But
neither did it dwindle in a fingersnap. They
joked and drew together, then some modicum of injured pride
in one or the other uncoupled them, and then they drew together again
—like magnets with their poles in erratic reversals, that's
the way I see my parents on this night so long ago,
I'm something floating in the iffy, misty realm
of possibility only. "Finally we were silly together.
We got out the dinner your mother had ruined—" "Had
ruined! I'll have you know—" "—and there were pieces of roast
so hard, like pucks, like *hockey pucks,* we sat down
on the kitchen floor and played checkers on its tiles."
Something sweet in this: my parents have always represented
the strengths of a standard middle-class family unity
that so many friends of my own have found elusive. And
one day, quite a while after my father was dead, my mother
(she must have already been in her seventies, I don't know *what*
sassy bug got into her) repeated the legend
and added, with a thespian wink, this ending line:
"*Strip* checkers." / And not only do we use them

to appease our gods—they *are* our gods. The bison
on the cave wall is depicted as the size of a typhoon,
and is a force that we could enter
and be transubstantiated. Also the cattle skulls
of Anatolia, reenfleshed with clay, and positioned
in shrines in the wall. The sacred Apis bull of ancient Egypt,
when it died, was embalmed with a process using
natron salts, and oil injected into the anus, and buried
in a sarcophagus of rose granite, and the mummy linen
adorned with gold, and the priests mourned sixty days,
and why?—"The Apis bull was said to be engendered by a ray of light
descending on a cow"; its soul was at one
with that of Osiris. And of the Yogi, Marco Polo says
"They worship the ox, and most of them carry a little ox
of gilt copper or bronze in the middle of the forehead.
They burn cow dung and make a powder of it, with this
they anoint various parts of their body with great reverence."
Someone making an ostentatiously splashy show of burning cow poop.
Someone else—an agéd, hump-bent woman let's say—
more modestly hobbling across the late, faint lilac shades of fading daylight
to her ancestors' graves; she carries a wooden bowl
with a symbolic cut of pork-fat in its center; and she kneels,
and feeds the dead, and makes the casual conversation
with them of an intimate talking to trusted friends.
All night, for long after the distant village candles darken,
they share the old tales. / My cousin Deedee
used to date (if that's the appropriate term)
a muscle-lumpy fuckrock bass guitarist given wholly over
to '60s-style neopimpflash clothes and peppermint schnapps
she'd pour at parties directly into his mouth
from hers, his fans all called him Dr. Meat;
but that, as my reticent family says when pressed,
is another story.

natural history

Natural History

1.

As for the elephant, "it is the largest of land animals"
(which is verifiably true), and "it mates in secret because
of its modesty" (debatable at best), and
"it is attested-to that an elephant has learned to write with its trunk
in Greek" (which is surely a ring-tailed doozy).
And an ox *can't* speak.
The bodies of crabs do *not* transform into scorpions during a drought.
And what of the "stars
that alight on the yardarms and other parts of a ship,
with a sound resembling a voice, and hopping
from perch to perch in the manner of birds"?—well, yes:
St. Elmo's fire, a "real" "phenomenon."
That's the way it always is with Pliny, and probably
everybody: first, the dry, inarguable display
of his metallurgical knowledge, term by term, ore by ore,
and before long "there are men with dog's heads"
introduced with insouciant assurance—"they bark
instead of speaking and live by hunting and fowling,
for which they use their nails." Pliny
inveigles—in*finagles*—our trust
by toe-dunk stages into the warm bathwater shallows of what's
soon oceanic depth. I've been in his books-length history over my head,
amid the snake that suckles at a cow's distended udders,
and the rain of milk and blood, and the Astomi
"who have no mouth, and so no food or drink,
but live from the emanations of flowers and apples that they carry
(they can be killed by a vigorous odor)." And:
"For speech, the dolphin moans like a human being."
T ( ) F ( )
"A copy of Homer's *Iliad* once was writ on parchment, small enough
so that it was stored inside a nutshell."

T ( )   F ( )
"The pelican feeds its young its breast-blood."
T ( )   F ( )
"The crocodile bird struts into that monster's gaping mouth
as it sleeps, and cleans its teeth and its throat."
T ( )   F ( )
"Through drinking of wine beyond a specific limit, the secrets
of the heart are revealed."
T ( )   F ( )
                    —And so
we see veracity is compromised by dubiousness
in increments as subtle as infant breath;
and only our own
nose-in-it experience is dependable
—if that.* *Do* I believe
that "boiled cabbage prevents insomnia"?
No—not at Casa Goldbarth, it doesn't. Do I believe
that "the eyes connect to the brain by a vein,
and also to the stomach"? Probably
—Goldbarth and Pliny say medical research
sorely lags behind in this embracingly explanatory notion.
And that "Marcus Lepidus . . . is known to have died
because of the stress occasioned by his divorce"?
Yes, *that,* at least, is ascertainable, *that* one verity
I can swear to. I have burned at the base of that great
asbestos heart, I have sat beneath the tree
whose seed is a flake of ash, its leaves are ashes,
and its flowers, I have sat in the ashen fall of its pollen
deadening the air. And there are friends of mine,
a painter of airy lakescapes and his mergers lawyer wife,
whose interior world just now, if translated
into the images of the nightly news, would be a nest of snipers
and the wounded being carried away in long lines over rocky ground.
"This alone is certain," Pliny says, "that there is no such thing
as certainty." Yes. And as for "the vapors
the Nile does" (or doesn't) "give off," and as for "the rays
like minds beam unto each other,"
I'm sorry but none of it,
no matter its attractions, is beyond sane disputation

————————————

*From a 1940s hard-boiled detective story: "He had gotten to the point where he didn't
believe what he heard even when he was talking to himself" (Norbert Davis).

. . . any more than the accepted definition of *I love you* is engraved
on a bar of plutonium in a hermetically sealed tubule of eterno-gas
in an underground vault in Stockholm
under Truth Police surveillance.
—No.

2.

The lake's an oolong brown today,
and gives itself away in rising mist. He views it
thoughtfully, this painter of water and shore; or
anyway, as thoughtfully as overriding marriage angsts allow.
And we can roll our eyes in tight ironic circles
at this common, sitcom-style brand of grief, but
no one's pain has ever registered
any less urgently for that. He thinks
Who's Right (or Wrong), Who's Guilty, Who's the Stinkeroo in All of This
—those categoried ponderings that seemed as architecturally defined
as a row of obelisks or equestrian statues
yesterday as they devastated each other with gall-and-adrenalin bombs,
but now . . . somehow . . . it's all more
like the lake, a scene of fog and indeterminacy,
a moil of accusation, noodgying, disaffection, and longing
they've been walking through as if through billowed haze
until they're both half-haze themselves. Now in the midst
of a life he once thought he could thunk with his knuckles
and hear ring back in an absolute way . . . today
he lifts his hand and almost sees it
flicker, reappear, then flicker once again. . . .

                                  And so tonight,
part-dozed on the back-room bed, he's not surprised
to see a smoky spectral-self rise out of himself
and float off, with an ever-extensive tendril
of smoky connection remaining between. (From Pliny:
"Hermotimus of Clazomenae used to leave his body
and wander about, reporting many things from afar.")
The journey is long and fast—the planet
smudges by, below—and then he lands at the edge of a meadow
men are walking across (it's late noon here), their catch
of wood duck and ptarmigan tied like skirts about their waists
. . . these snouted men with the sensitive, tentlike ears.
He's here in the land of the Dogfaces. Wow.

                                  They lead him,
not ungently, to their village (his necessary thread
of attachment-back-to-home still trailing from him). None
speaks "words," but they have throaty rumbles, aspirates, and yips
that are clearly a pliant and intricate language. Soon
he learns to distinguish individual members of the packtribe;
and, as in the world he comes from, brutish looks can hide
a sympathetic heart, or open faces mask conniving.

He meets the sachem of these people, a gaunt and ocher-eyed
old dogman; and he's given a room in the sachem's
sprawling mega-hut, with walls of mud-daub thatch
made appealing by tapestries showing hunting scenes,
some amorous entwinings (a tug of the home-thread here,
a sad, insistent tug), and what appears to be war
with a scatter of humanoid enemies. He never "gets"
their other-larynxed language, quite, and yet a mix
of body-moves, goodwill, and mutual grunts and sighs
allows him understanding enough to walk the village
comfortably and accepted.
                            With the royal house's
seneschal he indulges in smoking "dream leaf"
out of a shallow-bowl ceremonial pipe. With the childrenpups
he chases ribboned hoops along the rough streets.
With the women he learns to pound meal. When the sachem's
lady (something like their queen) falls ill with fever,
he's able to ease her plight by humming TV theme songs
at her cot. The sachem's concern is a grave
and admirable thing. (So then, again, that gossamer
pull of his "real body," toward his "real home.")
                                        One night
he sees the warriors stuffing woven bags with shit.
A truce is broken, they're at war once more
with their age-old foes the Astomi—who are fierce and sly,
but pungent smells will fell them as surely as spears will.
He can join the men in battle, but first he needs initiation
at the god-hut, to symbolically remove the skins
of his earlier life—the mall-skin (*hei!*)
and the clock-skin (*hei!*) and the job-skin (*hei!*)
and the book-skin (*hei!*) and the wife-skin
—and before he can tell them *no!* the home-thread
snaps; and he's abandoned here.
                              Do *you* believe in "the rays
like minds beam unto each other"? He
still doesn't fully understand their doggish talk,
but some days it's as if he's stopped at a light
and one of the Dogfaces pulls up right alongside,
they're listening to the same song on the radio,
both singing it, both of them seeing
that they're singing it, so singing it louder
and crazier, rocking the wheels now, *baby, oh, oh, bay-beee,*
howling it, and howling it.

3.

Do *you* believe
that Danny Harper, blind for sixteen years,
regained his sight "when he was hit on the head
by a falling chicken carcass"? * — *Well,*
maybe. In any case, my friend, the *Daily Telegraph,*
Europa Times, and the *Daily Mirror* reported this.
Do you believe that lightning fatally blasted a woman
in Scotland when it hit her metal-wire-reinforced bra?
Okay; why not? Do you believe her name
is Elotta Watts? *No I don't; do you?*
I'm reserving judgment. Do you believe
it bounced from her and struck her friend
who had been confined to a wheelchair from multiple sclerosis
for twenty-four years, and she rose to her feet and walked?
—a Mary Stryke. *That crosses the line.*
What *is* the line? The little green men. . . .
The fall of raw meat from out of a clear blue sky. . . .
"I do not for a flame-ass minute believe
my own seventeen-year-old daughter is capable of driving
a stolen vehicle *at all,* much less a car
with a thousand dollars of stolen jewelry in the trunk,"
said Lady Kaye, the topless dancer at Obsessions,
in a fluid mix of tequila and tears, and with
such monolithic conviction as surely withstands
the scowls of the dunderheadedly doubtful,
why?—do *you* not believe it?
Angels. Water of Lourdes. Perdition. Antimatter.
Satan. Neutrinos. In Omiya, a suburb of Tokyo,
"in 16 separate incidents, 150 pigs' heads
have been found by puzzled residents." "BullSHIT,"
he says, "if you think I'M going to swallow
men ever walked on no moon." We can only
keep our credibility wary (open),
open (wary), and walk the dappled light of our time
with a show of appropriate
wonder.
          "The one who wonders,"
Admirans, is what the king of Spain as a joke suggested

---

*It smelled a bit off, said the woman who'd dropped it from her tenth-floor apartment.

Columbus should be called (instead of *Almirante,*
"the admiral")—such was the effect
of the seemingly endless New World marvels
on his toughened sensibility;
yes, empirically pragmatic though his purpose was, Columbus goes
continuously gaga over every further twist of possibility
on these shores. It's from about this time
the notion of a "curio"—a souvenir of grandeur or of freakishness—
is born; and *fifteen centuries*
after that oh-so-compendious Roman observer's inaccuracies,
the pastor/explorer Jean de Léry in 1578 could say
"I have revised the opinion I formerly had of Pliny
and others when they describe foreign lands, because
[he's just returned from Brazil] I have seen things as fantastic
and prodigious as any of those—once thought
incredible—that they mention."
If the rhinoceros: why *not* the unicorn?
If the manatee: why not the merfolk?
If the flying squirrel: the griffin, the roc.
The armadillo: *anything.*
Is a buffalo any stranger than a basilisk is, *really?*
Or for that matter, is the amoeba?
is the ovary?
are your spouse's dreams?
                              Do you believe these marriages
announced in daily papers?—Storm-Flood;
Beers-Franks; Long-Cox; Sharpe-Payne; Stock-King;
Good-Loser. I've seen the clippings. Do you believe *this*
marriage?—annulled in 1995, when one Bruce Jensen
of Bountiful, Utah, discovered Leasa Bibianna Herrera,
his wife since 1991, was truly Felix Urioste, a man
who "had enrolled as a female student
at the University of Utah and had worked as a doctor
in four Salt Lake City hospitals, alternating
between male and female aliases" (The *Fortean Times,*
as culled from the *Ogden (UT) Standard-Examiner* and *Meriden (CT) Record-Journal).*
Ah!—there is no woolly poppycock, no tommyrot flambé,
to match the straight-to-the-astonishment-gland details
of actual happenstance. One of the Egyptian king Merneptah's
victory monuments in 1300 B.C. lists 13,240
severed penises from conquered Libyans, Etruscans, and Greeks
presented as trophies. / Lee Herman, entomologist:
"We sometimes dissect insects under a microscope

with scalpels we make from tiny pins. Sometimes
the pulse in your thumb will cause the scalpel to jump. . . .
You learn to dissect between heartbeats." / "The gecko's
[pupil] looks like a string of four diamonds, the skate's
a fan-shaped Venetian blind, the fire-bellied toad
an opening like a piece of pie, the armored catfish a horseshoe,
the penguin a star that tightens into a square, the green whip snake
a keyhole, and others resemble teardrops,
bullets, buns, crescent moons, hearts, hourglasses, boomerangs" (Guy Murchie).

So why do we heap such retrospect contumely on this man
who said that "lettuces . . . increase the volume of blood,"
who said "the hair will grow on a corpse," and who,
among his best encyclopedic tries, gave us the manticore:
"the face of a man, a lion's body, a tail like a scorpion's"
—in *this* life, in *this* world,
a not unthinkable proposition.

4.

As to painters' verisimilitude, Pliny tells us:
"In a contest between Zeuxis and Parrhasius," the former
"produced so successful a representation of grapes
that birds flew up to feast there." Plump with pride
at this deception, Zeuxis very disdainfully indicates
the curtain hung in front of his competitor's inferior entry
now be drawn aside—*then* realizes the curtain *is* the painting;
"and he conceded the prize."
                                        My wife says
"You're not *listening* to me," when of course I am,
I'm just not *agreeing* with her. This
makes her mightily pissed, and I can't blame her:
all of us, everybody, little two-bit
zeuxises and parrhasiuses, expecting
that *our* version of reality will be,
in any contest, all-persuasive. This explains
the martial loggerheads of nation-states,
as well as the deep assumption behind most "couples counseling,"
sure; and even so, such knowledge doesn't assuage
a man up walking late one post-misunderstanding night,
a man who's tossed in the crosscurrents ambience
of totaling his transgressions, and hers (first gingerly
separating them out from each other) . . . if he's anything
like me, he'll stare this conscienceful endeavor
straight in its stony face, and try, he'll *really*
try . . . but after a difficult while of ethics,
anger, melancholia, the heebie-jeebies, sneers, nobility,
mean-spiritedness, and sighs, it segues
into escapist fancies. . . .
                                        He's an artist,
remember. So here's what he does. With globby smears
of animal fats and oils as a base, he trial-and-errors together
a make-do range of paints by mixing-in various berry juices
and riverbank clays. The hairs and handles for some brushes
aren't difficult to rig, and he talks the tribal skinner
out of a tattered length of her scraped, tanned hides,
that he primes with his own chalk goo concoction. Now
he's ready. One night he slinks off to the woods-edge
with his tools and enough for a stuttery, furtive fire.
Goodbye, you Dogface-ones. Goodbye, goodbye.
Even as he works, he looks toward the village with something

akin to fondness: not an obviating fondness, no,
but a real one nonetheless. And after several
strenuous hours, he's completed a miniature version of his body,
stretched as if in sleep, and done impeccably
trompe l'oeil . . .
                and he funnels back
into it, back in time, and place,
and materializes—*corporealizes*—back
in their own late twentieth-century troubled American bed.

5.

She's a mergers lawyer, remember.
That's an expertise as unyielding to me as brick
or an understanding of escrow. I can't even claim
much access to her dream life, to her wishes
—I'm weary with discord of my own today,
and far from any authorly omniscience. But
I *do* know—it's easy to see, by a flicker of pensive wryness
over her face as she kills time sorting bric-a-brac
in the attic, in its dim watts—that she finds it
especially ironic, the "mergers" part at which
she's supposedly so damn blow-your-eyes-out good;
not in this house, she isn't, they aren't, not
at merging lately in any viable way. And yet . . .
She idly flips through a stack of his unframed canvases.
This one, the day the lake became a steaming witches' cauldron,
or a kettle of fuming hobo stew. . . . And *this* one,
she remembers the day, they'd had a vivifying if cheap
white wine and cajun sausage, and he'd showed her
how the "blue" of it was dozens of colors, really,
if you really looked. . . . She knows
that you can't love a man for his art any more
than for a tight tush or a fatass roll of banknotes.
Still, . . . (*and now she's lost in reverie*) . . .
She has /not good but hopeful/ news from the clinic
about the lump. *He used to hum those TV theme songs*
by my side when I took sick
until I smiled through the hurt. And she goes downstairs
to the back-room bed as he opens his eyes from sleep,
and he says—*a weird thing, almost*
as if he'd been away on a journey—
"I'm back home now."

∽

What *are* we going to do with that man?
He'll feed us any gee-whiz scrap of balderdash
and he won't go away, he won't remove
his ancient foot from the door of the twenty-first century,*

---

* From the February 5, 1996, issue of *Time:* "Writing his *Natural History* in the first century A.D.,

he knows the tiny oh-wow-bone in our ears
is evolved exactly to relay /*zap zap zap*/ astonishment
that the other bones, the payroll-bones and the mortgage-bones,
reject. Because of him I've looked in a woman's face
and seen the ox that speaks,
and the people who turn into wolves, and the bees
that by their flight predict the future.
I've looked in the mirror and seen
the proof of that great truth of his,
"the heart is the seat of the mind."
The two-inch goby fish attaches to a rudder
and stalls a galley ship of four hundred rowers.
The human embryo wears hair, like a beast.
The Arimaspi have but one eye; that, in the middle of the forehead.
There are days when I can almost believe
the marriage will last, will seam itself
and last, and stars will sing of this
to starfish, in the language that they share
because they share a shape.

~

Today they browse together through one of his books
of fifteenth-century art. The anonymous painter
shows us Pliny's dog-faced tribe the only way he knows:
as credibly rendered, yes
and set with weight and history and desires
in the hill-land of a credibly rendered world.
They trade their formulaic greetings and they sell their busheled grain
no more implausibly
than the hundreds of thousands of fifteenth-century saints
conduct *their* nimbused business.

Pliny the Elder reported that when water rises into the atmosphere to form rain clouds, it
sucks up with it shoals of fish and sometimes quantities of stones. Fish and stones hover
above us in the sky. Elsewhere, Pliny offered an item about a woman who gave birth to an
elephant. He was, occasionally, a supermarket-tabloid sort of Roman. A Pliny pattern persists.
The scientific side of the observer's mind demands objective evidence, as the great naturalist
usually did; but the brain's mythopoeic, magic-thinking side is lured to marvels—to alchemy,
to spells, to bat people on the moon or aliens on other planets. Can these matters be ad-
dressed with a whole mind? Can the two instincts of the brain—Einstein and Elvis-sighting—
be made to fit together like compatible spoons?" (Lance Morrow).

On the next page, a companion piece—and equally
convincing: Pliny's
                    "headless people,
they have their eyes in their shoulders, and their mouths in their chests."
And once we're past a sort of pink cartoonishness
attending them, we see that they're complete
unto their needs and their fashions—simpering, valorous,
dour, gleeful, every one of them
somebody's child, somebody's neighbor,
every one of them rumpled at night one way or another
by love. The nipple-level smiles are genuine
endorsements of a happiness, for some; while others
wear theirs as a burglar might his mask.
Some are slovenly, others are dapper; voluptuary;
teetotaling;—consider the spectrum of "character"
run through fully. They argue the merits of the printing press,
and other abrupt newfangledness. They can't
believe it. They rumormonger. They have
their dragons and seraphs and pucks. A few of them
are walking out of the frame of the painting
hand in hand, among the lemon-yellow flower-bearing trees
and spaghetti-like grasses, they're going to test the line
between endurance and mismatchment.
Haven't we all, at some time, lost our heads?
They go their own encoded way,
like any confused human beings.

Albert Goldbarth is the author of several volumes of poetry, including *Popular Culture, Marriage, and Other Science Fiction,* and *Adventures in Ancient Egypt.* He is the recipient of numerous awards, among them the National Book Critics Circle Award, a Guggenheim fellowship, fellowships from the National Endowment for the Arts, the Chad Walsh Memorial Award, and the Ohio State University Press/*The Journal* Award in Poetry. He is currently Distinguished Professor of Humanities in the Department of English at Wichita State University.